D1164414

Affairs

Affairs

A Guide to Working Through the Repercussions of Infidelity

Emily M. Brown

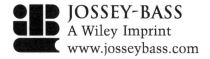

JOSSEY-BASS
A Wiley Imprint
www.josseybass.com

Published by

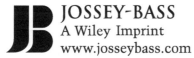

JOSSEY-BASS
A Wiley Imprint
www.josseybass.com

Jossey-Bass books and products are available through most bookstores. To contact Jossey-Bass directly, call (888) 378-2537, fax to (800) 605-2665, or visit our website at www.josseybass.com.

Substantial discounts on bulk quantities of Jossey-Bass books are available to corporations, professional associations, and other organizations. For details and discount information, contact the special sales department at Jossey-Bass.

We at Jossey-Bass strive to use the most environmentally sensitive paper stocks available to us. Our publications are printed on acid-free recycled stock whenever possible, and our paper always meets or exceeds minimum GPO and EPA requirements.

Library of Congress Cataloging-in-Publication Data

Brown, Emily M. Affairs: a guide to working through the repercussions of infidelity / Emily M. Brown. — 1st. ed.
    p. cm.
  Includes bibliographical references and index.
  ISBN 0-7879-5004-1 (alk. paper)
1. Adultery. 2. Marriage—Psychological aspects. I. Title.
HQ806 .B76 1999
306.73'6—dc21   99-6189

FIRST EDITION
HB Printing   10 9 8 7 6 5 4 3

Contents

Preface

My interest in affairs developed years ago from my growing aware-ness as a therapist and family mediator that affairs don't necessar-ily mean divorce. In fact, I saw many affairs serve as marital turning points, challenging couples to resolve long-standing issues. And I saw many divorces occur without an affair. I learned that the affair that is quickly followed by divorce is usually the vehicle for ending the marriage, not the reason. Whatever the outcome of an affair, the experience is emotionally difficult for those involved.

It was only later that I realized that I was intrigued by affairs at a much deeper level, having to do with the pain of betrayal that we each experience in growing up. Affairs are a powerful metaphor for betrayals of all sorts, and we resonate with them based on our prior experience with betrayal. Even when we are not directly involved, learning about an affair stirs up painful memories of past betrayals, and reminds us that we are not immune.

The terminology I use, *betrayed spouse* and *betraying spouse,* is not meant to blame or exonerate either spouse. Rather, these labels reflect our culture's lack of nonjudgmental language about affairs. I have chosen *betrayed* and *betraying* because betrayal is the motif I hear most often from my clients during the early stages of talking about their own experience.

Affairs occur in the context of a commitment to be monoga-mous. The commitment may be verbal or nonverbal, but it is clear to both partners. This commitment has not been renegotiated. When an affair presents itself in your life or in the life of someone close to you, it creates an upsetting emotional puzzle. Most people don't expect that they or their partners will become involved in an affair. If an affair occurs (and chances are it will as 70 percent of marriages experience at least one affair), they don't know what to do.[1] This book offers guidance for those whose life is touched by an affair:

- The betrayed spouse
- The betraying spouse
- The third party
- Children, family, and friends

Betrayals always elicit strong emotions; when the betrayal is sexual, emotions escalate rapidly. Some of the common emotional responses to an affair create barriers to understanding and working on the issues that led to the affair. This book is designed to help readers move beyond those barriers, freeing them to address old issues and learn new skills. Couples in committed relationships, married or not, straight or gay, can use the information presented here to better understand how the stage was set for an affair and to address the deeper issues in their relationship.

You might think of an affair as notice that it is time to rebuild the relationship on firmer ground. To use the opportunity presented by this crisis, those involved need to understand what is happening and know how to move ahead.

Affairs
- Offers step-by-step guidance for facing the affair and resolving the real problems underlying the affair.
- Provides a safe context in which to explore affairs, uncontaminated by moral, religious, or gender judgments.
- Demystifies the myths about what happens after an affair.
- Helps readers identify the nature of their own situation so that they can begin addressing the tasks of healing.
- Facilitates honest dialogue between the spouses.

- Guides couples who are committed to their marriage through the tasks of healing and rebuilding trust.
- Guides those whose marriage is ending through the practical and emotional tasks of healing and moving on.
- Offers guidance for talking with children, family, and friends.
- Provides a road map of the steps to forgiveness.

The guidance offered here is based on my work over twenty-five years with couples and individuals who have struggled with the issues presented by an affair. Many of these couples used the affair as the catalyst to build a much better marriage than they had prior to the affair. Their courage in facing the affair and addressing their hidden dilemmas provided the energy to turn their marriage around. Others who were not able to rebuild their marriage worked just as hard to come to terms with the affair, their spouse, and themselves as they rebuilt their lives and moved toward forgiveness. Children whose parents helped them cope with a parental affair came through this difficult experience intact. Unmarried third parties also have issues to address; with courage and hard work, they do so successfully. The key to a positive outcome is in facing the situation and accepting the challenge of healing old wounds and learning new skills so that the future will be different from the past.

You too have the chance to use the affair as a catalyst for moving your life in new and more positive directions. My hope for you is that you will be courageous in converting this crisis into an opportunity for making changes that let you be truly yourself in an intimate relationship.

June 1999

Emily M. Brown
Arlington, Virginia

Acknowledgments

It took many people to write this book, even though I am the only author named. Many people contributed by sharing their personal stories, others expanded my thinking, some critiqued the manuscript, and still others offered encouragement and support.

My appreciation goes first to those from whom I have learned so much: those who shared with me their personal experience with an affair. They include my clients, the participants in my research on children of affairs, and others who were generous in describing to me their situations, their struggles, and their views about the aftereffects of the affairs in their lives. My thinking has also been stimulated by the questions and comments of therapists participating in my workshops, throughout the country and internationally, on how to work with clients' affairs.

The encouragement of friends and colleagues has been extremely important, particularly when publishers insisted that people would be too embarrassed to be seen buying a book on affairs. Not only have these friends and colleagues shared my excitement about this book, but many reviewed the manuscript and made invaluable suggestions. They include Linda Girdner, Peter Maida, Betsy Mandel-Carley, Venus Masselam, Isolina Ricci, and Bob Rix. Venus, who has a wonderful way of using words, helped me with the comments that begin each chapter. Marcia Lebowitz contributed by challenging my thinking in very helpful ways. Dick Anderson, Karen Smith, and Diane Wiltjer have been supportive and encouraging throughout. Michael LeClair has been creative in developing my Web site, www.affairs-help.com, which provides me with continual feedback from men and women who are struggling with the aftermath of an affair.

To my great joy, my editor at Jossey-Bass, Leslie Berriman, saw the need for this book the moment she first read the manuscript. She has shared her excitement about the book with me and has guided me in making the text flow smoothly. Others at Jossey-Bass who have helped bring this book to fruition include Joanne Clapp Fullagar, Paula Goldstein, Katie Crouch, Margaret Sebold, Lisa Shannon, Cris Cooke, and Kim Corbin.

My deep appreciation goes to all the contributors to this book.

Affairs

Chapter One

The Five Types of Affairs

Affairs are never foreign, but as with our local
rivers, they vary in their origins and destinations.

Affairs are powerful and primal. Any betrayal raises questions about
trust and the values we live by, but sexual betrayals strike deep
emotional chords having to do with love and abandonment,
thrilling fantasies and worst fears, and our own dark side and that
of our partner. Because the emotions roused by an affair are so primal, it is difficult to understand what an affair really means.

Different affairs mean different things. They're never just about
sex! They're not about loving or not loving your spouse! They're
about finding a way to feel alive in the face of discomfort or pain,
or when you don't know how to get a handle on what's going on
with you or your marriage.

Our sexuality gives us a way of communicating at an intimate
level. We can use sex to let our partner know we care, to feel close,
to express passion and any number of other things. We can also use
sex to send messages about issues other than sex or intimacy. This is
the nature of affairs. They send a message about pain and discomfort.

Many husbands and wives don't know how to get below the surface to what's driving or disturbing them. Each is desperately searching for a way out of the pain and confusion. When words and
understanding aren't available, spouses resort to more primitive and
therefore more passionate means of speaking about their wounds.
Each type of affair protects against a particular type of pain. The pain
may be related to fears of conflict or of intimacy, to feeling empty at

the core, to being torn between shoulds and wants, or to trepidation about endings. Affairs send a message to a partner about the pain, although it is a message that a partner has trouble decoding.

Affair patterns are much like dances. In some dances both partners execute the same steps, while in others each partner has a different but reciprocal set of steps. So it is with affairs. In some types of affairs the patterns of the husband and wife are similar, in others the patterns differ—but always they are reciprocal. It is the pattern of behavior between the husband and wife that indicates the type of affair, not just the behavior of the partner having the affair.

Laurie's affair is a way of letting her husband know how dissatisfied she is. Ken's affair indicates that he is torn within himself between taking care of others and taking care of himself. Paula's affair means she is leaving her marriage. Your affair or your partner's may be different from any of these—and it doesn't have to mean divorce! It does mean there is a problem—a problem that goes deeper than the affair.

When you don't understand the message it is tempting to get into blaming or fixing—or both. Understanding the meaning of the affair in your life will help you make sane decisions during this crazy time. Understanding the affair means becoming aware of who you really are. Resolving the affair means making conscious choices about how you live your life.

The guidelines presented here suggest positive paths through the pain and anger and bewilderment that accompany an extramarital affair. They are based on my work with thousands of people who have successfully faced an affair and struggled through to a new understanding of themselves and their marriage. This book will help you talk about what has happened, work through your pain, resist impulsive actions that you might regret, and move toward healing and forgiveness. Along the way you will explore a variety of issues that need to be resolved. Reading this book may help you salvage your relationship, or it may help you end your marriage with dignity. At the very least, it can help you reclaim your self—essential if you don't want to repeat this painful experience in the future.

First, we're going to look at the different types of affairs and what they mean. Then we will focus on dos and don'ts for getting you through the crisis of disclosure in one piece. Next is examining each step along the path ahead of you: the pain, the opportunities, the traps, the decision points, and ways to achieve resolution and forgiveness. We'll also explore how you can help your children through this crisis, ways to deal with the reactions of your friends and relatives, motivations of unmarried third parties, and considerations when violence is a possibility.

As you read about the five types of affairs, see if you can identify which of the following patterns fits your situation.

The Conflict Avoidance Affair

You know the Conflict Avoiders—they're that nice couple up the street who never fight. In reality they're terrified to be anything but nice for fear that conflict will lead to abandonment or losing control. They don't have a way to stand up to each other when there's a problem, so they can't resolve their differences and the marriage erodes.

Profile of Conflict Avoiders

- Either the husband or the wife is having an affair, not both.
- The spouse who is having the affair feels guilty.
- The affair usually comes within the first ten or so years of the marriage.
- The affair is short-lived.
- Both spouses tend to be overly nice and helpful, whether they feel like it or not.
- Irritation is expressed, but open conflict is avoided. When differences surface, the subject is dropped and the issue is left unresolved.
- Valued elements of the marriage have been eroding because of the couple's inability to discuss and resolve their differences.
- The pair are often seen by their friends as a model couple.

- Stresses such as pregnancy and the arrival of children, combined with the inability to discuss differences, have shifted the focus away from the husband-wife relationship.

The Origins of Conflict Avoidance Affairs

We learn about close relationships early in life from our families. We learn whether it is safe to be emotionally vulnerable, whether to accommodate, to fight or to flee, whether feelings are valued or feared, how honest to be, and what to hide. We bring these patterns to our relationships. These patterns can keep us unaware of our own feelings and motivations. Whatever we're unaware of in ourselves provides fertile ground for an affair.

Laurie, twenty-eight, and Arthur, thirty-five, have been married for five years. Laurie learned early in life to avoid conflict. Her mom always cautioned her, "Don't be so selfish. Just overlook it. Your sister didn't mean it, so you don't need to get so upset." Laurie's family has a "nice" facade, but inside the tension is high because issues get buried instead of being resolved. In a sense, members of families like Laurie's are handicapped when it comes to handling differences of opinion.

Laurie married Arthur because she saw him as strong and self-assured. These days she resents his dominance. Arthur was originally attracted by Laurie's desire to please him, but now he is frustrated by her unwillingness to tell him what she wants.

Laurie confides to her friend, "Arthur is a really good person, and I don't want to upset him over every little thing. It's really not that important." But she mopes around. Arthur tells his racquetball partner, "I don't know what's gotten into her—maybe it's just a female thing—I can't get a word out of her!" At home he is impatient and quick with his decisions, seldom checking with Laurie any more.

Both of them are resentful, but both suppress their feelings because as kids they learned, "Don't say anything that you wouldn't want said to you," and "Real men don't get petty." Neither knows how to talk about anger or pain and they are afraid that saying the wrong thing will stir up trouble. Besides, if something was really off base, wouldn't the other say so? They continue their dance of pleasantries and ignore their growing feelings of discomfort.

Laurie and Arthur are classic Conflict Avoiders. It is not that they never feel angry or annoyed, but they always let the issue drop so as to avoid any open conflict. Moreover, they don't know how to share their uncomfortable feelings with each other—and they don't realize that it is important to do so. Both need a way to reach the other. Laurie gets Arthur's attention when he picks up the phone, overhears Laurie's conversation with Brad, and discovers she is having an affair.

Are You and Your Partner Conflict Avoiders?

If you are like Laurie and Arthur, you don't like to argue, so you go out of your way to accommodate each other, even though you can get very annoyed. Not fighting is a source of pride: you can rise above the "small stuff"; you can protect your spouse from any unnecessary pain. Of course a lot of things don't get discussed, but you tell yourself, "They're not important, I can put them behind me. I'll do whatever's necessary to keep things running smoothly." Meanwhile all the little "unimportant" stuff accumulates, weighing you down as you worry alone.

You are probably in the first ten or so years of your marriage. You care about your spouse, but you feel frustrated by the loss of romance and the dailyness that has set in. Since the baby came, it's been rough. No time for romantic dinners, for leisurely sex, or even taking a shower in peace. Dissatisfaction hovers like a low gray cloud, but you push it into the background. You believe in marriage. And you don't know what else to do!

The Intimacy Avoidance Affair

Intimacy Avoiders are couples who are frightened of intimacy, of being emotionally vulnerable, so they keep the barriers high between them. Fighting is one barrier; affairs are another. The emotional connection between the spouses is through frequent and intense battles, usually verbal and sometimes accentuated by slamming doors or other dramatic actions. In some cases these fights escalate into physical violence. These couples are the mirror opposite of the Conflict Avoiders—it's fight instead of flight. Although any kind of affair indicates some problem with intimacy, with these couples, intimacy is *the* issue.

Profile of Intimacy Avoiders

- Both partners fear intimacy, and set up barriers to keep from feeling too close.
- The spouses confuse closeness with feeling trapped.
- The couple gets into frequent escalating fights, with a lot of blaming and fault-finding.
- The fights are intense.
- The emotional connection between the partners is through fighting.
- Often both partners are having affairs.
- The partners are usually in their twenties and thirties and have been married less than six years before the first affair, or they are in the early years of a subsequent marriage.
- The affair is of relatively brief duration.
- The affair is not kept secret for long.
- Each spouse grew up in a family that was disorganized or chaotic, possibly with an alcoholic or abusive parent.

The Origins of Intimacy Avoidance Affairs

Colleen has been married to Will for five years now. Colleen responded to Will's recent affair with one of her own. In Colleen's family, fighting was the usual mode for approaching differences. Her mother is an alcoholic who alternated between rage and affection throughout Colleen's childhood. Her father's frequent verbal harangues toward her mother were interspersed with "kiss and make up" periods. He finally gave up and left the family when Colleen was fourteen, leaving her to deal from day to day with her mother's alternating moods. Colleen left home as soon as her younger sister was sixteen and could drive.

Disorganization was the modus operandi for Will's family. Little planning was done, routine tasks were skipped, and decisions were postponed for a better day. Whenever problems developed, there was an emotional explosion. Will learned to keep his distance and to fend for himself.

When Colleen and Will met, she was twenty-two and he was twenty-seven. He was drawn to her lively personality. She was attracted to his independence. They married five months after meeting. The first few months of marriage went reasonably well, but as they settled in they developed a pattern of snapping quickly, making accusations, and arguing frequently. They justified their attacks on each other, neither realizing that their real fear was of being vulnerable because it was so identified with pain.

After one of their bigger fights, Will went to the health club to work off his anger. He confided his discontent to a woman there and began an affair with her that night. Within six weeks he had "accidentally" left enough clues that Colleen discovered the affair. When she confronted Will, he admitted to the affair, but blamed Colleen, "I wouldn't need to look elsewhere if you weren't always attacking me." Colleen was furious and a blow-out fight followed. In the next few days, all her friends heard the details of what had happened as Colleen recruited them to take her side. Will told Colleen that she was being unreasonable, "It wasn't that big a deal." A bit later Colleen told herself, "What's good for one is good for the other. I'll show him how this really feels."

Even though Colleen and Will are fighting about his affair, they are still focused on each other. The affair is a way of communicating with each other, and not a relationship in and of itself. Will's message to Colleen is "back off." In a sense, he is acting on behalf of Colleen as well, since neither of them can tolerate being too close. Now, of course, Colleen's worst fears about intimacy are reinforced. Her retaliatory affair is an effort to avoid old feelings of abandonment, but it serves to reactivate Will's old fears. Their arguments increase and are focused on the affairs.

As things get out of hand, Colleen and Will get frightened and reach out to make peace with each other. They have a wonderfully intense sexual reconciliation and decide they will let the past be the past. They put their nagging fears aside in the interest of making things work. Their doubts come out as criticism of the other about little matters, another distancing technique. When they begin to feel uncomfortably close again, one or the other will provoke another fight. This cycle may lead to another affair. Colleen and Will are not consciously aware that these are distancing maneuvers, and they would tell you that they love each other and want to be close.

Colleen and Will have a lot of work to do if they are going to create an emotionally safe and loving marriage. They bring a lot of energy to the task, but they will need to redirect their energy from fighting to talking about how they really feel. They need to understand and talk about why intimacy is so scary for each of them and learn gradually how to risk being emotionally vulnerable with each other. Although they fight, they have no idea how to fight effectively. Learning the art of negotiation and developing healthy ways of moving closer and apart will be another part of the work ahead. If they are willing to do this work, they have the potential for constructing a marriage that is more intimate and less conflictual.

Are You and Your Partner Intimacy Avoiders?

If you're an Intimacy Avoider, you fear closeness more than conflict. You want intimacy, but it's just too scary. In the past, letting your guard down resulted in feeling trapped, getting hurt, or even being abandoned. When random life events don't provide a buffer, you find other means to protect yourself. Fighting is your first line of defense when your partner is getting too close. These fights are emotionally intense. It's as if all the emotions between you and your spouse are invested in fighting. And the fights never get settled, so it's easy to pick up again whenever you need to.

Your fights are about anything and everything. Anybody who is present and willing will get drawn into your fight. You ask your friends to take sides or to proclaim that you are right. Having an affair escalates the fight. Then you and your spouse fight about the affair. Your partner may retaliate with an affair. The emotional intensity of your fights increases and even though you're exhausted, you can't let go. Your emotional connection is through the fighting.

Neither of you really likes to fight. Below the surface is a great deal of pain and fear. Each of you wants the other to say "I really want to be with you," but when things are going well, you get scared. So both of you thrust and parry, back off, and then threaten with someone or something else. Your affair is a great buffer. At the same time you remain connected to your partner by the push-pull of the conflict.

The Sexual Addiction Affair

Sexual Addicts use sex over and over again to numb their inner pain and fill up the emptiness inside, much as alcoholics use alcohol. Among married people, men are sexual addicts more often than women. Many wives will tolerate a sexually addicted spouse but husbands generally will not. With Conflict Avoiders and Intimacy Avoiders, both partners have similar styles of interaction. With Sexual Addiction, each spouse has a different role: one engages in the addictive behavior, while the other enables that behavior. For each, their role provides a way to avoid pain and emptiness.

Profile of Sexual Addicts

- The Sexual Addict has had twenty-five, fifty, or more affairs.
- The seduction is as important as the affair, if not more so.
- The Sexual Addict has little, if any, relationship with the affair partner.

- The Sexual Addict turns to sex when feeling lonely, empty, in pain, or otherwise uncomfortable.
- The Sexual Addict denies that the behavior is a problem, even though shame may be experienced after the sexual encounter.
- A predictable cycle of behavior repeats from one sexual encounter to the next.
- Addiction to another escape, such as alcohol or pornography, is part of the pattern.
- The Sexual Addict doesn't bother hiding the sexual behavior.

Profile of Sexual Addicts' Spouses

- The spouse puts up with the Sexual Addict's behavior.
- The spouse presents a brave face to the outside world.
- The partners live rather separate lives.
- The spouse makes it easy for the Sexual Addict to pursue sexual conquests because the spouse is willing to carry responsibility that isn't his or hers.

The Origins of Sexual Addiction

Sexual addiction is often viewed as a joke, as a ridiculous idea, or as nonexistent. It is seen as an excuse to be promiscuous, or dismissed with the idea that the addict is "oversexed." But sexual addiction is real. It is not about sex, however, nor is it about romantic love. Charlotte Kasl, a psychologist, says, "Sexually addicted adults are essentially children hiding out in grown-up bodies, hungrily seeking parents to love them unconditionally."[1] Sexual addiction becomes understandable when we realize it results from severe abuse or neglect in early childhood, which has left the addict with painful wounds and an empty feeling inside. Sex becomes a way of anesthetizing the pain or of filling the emptiness, at least for a brief moment. Sexual addiction can take many forms, but our focus here is on the compulsive use of affairs.

Ed's family background is a common one among sexual addicts. Ed is forty-four and has been married to Michelle for twenty years. Ed's mother was the dominant influence in the family, since his father was seldom home. She turned to Ed, the youngest of her three sons, for companionship. She indulged Ed but the price she exacted was constant attention to her needs and her feelings. She was somewhat seductive in her physical affection, touching and hugging Ed and flirting with him as one would with a lover. Ed liked being her favorite, although he often felt confused. As a teen, he was revved up sexually by some of his mother's seductive behavior. He turned his sexual energy toward the females he met, enjoying the excitement of the chase and the seduction, but never wanting a serious relationship with them. Ed has continued his pattern of seduction through his courtship and marriage, until now.

Michelle alternates between covering up for Ed and badgering him in an effort to get him to change his ways. She works at keeping up a respectable facade, pretends that Ed's irregular hours are because of his work, and stays busy with the kids so that she doesn't have to feel. Her mother did much the same with her father's drinking.

Jean also uses sex to escape from her pain and emptiness, but her background is a bit different. She was sexually abused as a very young child by her mother's boyfriend. Jean's mother refused to listen to Jean or to see Jean's obvious fright. Jean was so traumatized that her unconscious mind has repressed the memory. She evolved into a sad and lonely child who was afraid of people. When Jean left home at the age of nineteen she began pursuing men and seducing them. It was almost as if she was recreating the very situation that had traumatized her as a child. She was ashamed but felt powerless to change her behavior.

When she got involved with Gary, who was crazy about her, she decided that marriage might dispel her need to be seductive. It hasn't helped—in fact, Jean is having a harder time suppressing her shame but she can't stop seducing the men who come her way. She worries about AIDS but continues behavior that she knows may destroy her marriage or her physical self.

Both Ed and Jean are Sexual Addicts. What they have in common is parents who paid no attention to their needs because they were so needy themselves. Neither Ed nor Jean got the nurturing care that allowed them to grow into secure adults. Ed got the message as a child that the way to get love is to be sexual. Jean is searching for someone to love her, and feels that sex is the necessary medium of exchange. For both Ed and Jean, sex, love, and pain have become intertwined and confused.

Is Sexual Addiction an Issue for You and Your Partner?

When you are addicted to affairs, you are obsessed with sexual conquests. You are unable to stop, even when your behavior is producing severe problems for you and may be life-threatening. You use sex as a brief fix for your pain and your shame. The high never lasts very long so you keep looking for the next fix, just like an alcoholic focuses on the next drink. Everything else comes second. You're so preoccupied that you don't take precautions against AIDS or other diseases.

If you are the spouse of someone who is a Sexual Addict, you go to great lengths to hide the addiction from others. Essentially you put up with your spouse's behavior, although you're on a crusade for him or her to change in some ways. By focusing on your spouse, you don't have to face your own issues—issues that are just as painful as the addict's.

The biggest difficulty for addicts and their spouses is the denial and the hiding, with the end result that you don't get the help you need to change. Both of you run the risk of continuing the cycle of compulsive sex (the addictive behavior) countered by efforts to manage it (enabling behavior) to fill your emptiness and avoid your pain. Because the roots of sexual addiction go so deep, both of you will need help in addressing your issues. This is not a do-it-yourself project. With help, it is possible to learn new patterns and to stop addictive and enabling behaviors.

The Split Self Affair

For Split Selves, the affair is about being fed up with doing marriage "right." Both you and your spouse have sacrificed your own feelings and needs to take care of others and the deprivation has been chilling. You're sick of it! The affair begins when someone comes along that stirs the vestiges of life in one of the partners. The affair is serious, long-term, and passionate. Once fully involved, the betraying partner struggles to decide between the spouse and the affair partner. Most often this is a man's affair, but more women than before are having these affairs.

This kind of affair is often regarded as a midlife crisis, but it is much more. The roots go back to pressures in childhood to meet the needs of others and put aside your own needs. In contrast, a midlife crisis is situational and develops with the awareness of time passing and things undone. Affairs during a midlife crisis are more likely to be Exit Affairs (see next section).

Profile of Split Selves

- Both partners have devoted themselves to doing what others want, especially what they think their family and children want.

- The couple has probably been married twenty years or more (although the discomfort comes sooner in some marriages).

- The couple has tried to build the right structure for their family.

- The partners are regarded as responsible and dependable by friends and colleagues.

- Each spouse views the other as controlling or demanding.

- As a child, neither partner was free to pursue their own needs and feelings, although they do not regard that as an important factor.

- At least one of the partners is depressed, and often both.

- You feel torn between your spouse and your affair partner, and you are trying to decide which one of them is right for you.
- You may have separated from your spouse but you missed your family and moved back in, only to find that you again want to leave.
- You are seeking passion in your life.

The Origins of Split Self Affairs

Ken, at forty-eight, has been having an affair for three years with Jill, who is thirty-one. He and his wife Phyllis, who is forty-seven, never dealt with a previous brief affair he had seven years into the marriage. Ken's affair with Jill is serious. His prior attempts to end it have failed, and for the past year and a half, the affair has proceeded parallel to the marriage. Ken doesn't flaunt his involvement with Jill, and for the most part makes some effort to be careful about where they go so that they don't bump into Phyllis. For her part, Phyllis tries to pretend that Jill doesn't exist. This time Phyllis can't put blinders on because Ken is about to move out again to be with Jill. He moved out once before, but missed his family and returned home.

Ken is troubled by his dishonesty and the burden of his double life. A classic "nice guy," he knows he is being anything but nice. He keeps attempting to decide which woman is the right woman for him, but his answer keeps switching back and forth. He has decided that what he needs to do now is act: "I just haven't been decisive enough. Moving in with Jill is the step I need to take. I'm sorry that Phyllis is hurt—I really don't want to hurt her, but this will be better for all of us."

Phyllis is panicked. Even though she has worked in recent years, her life has revolved around taking care of her family, especially her children. She is angry, upset, depressed, and hoping against hope that Ken will come to his senses. The idea of being totally alone frightens her to the core. She does everything she can think of to influence Ken to stay: sending him cards at his office, losing weight, asking him to tell her what he would like her to do, and trying to predict and meet every possible need of his. Ken feels pressured and backs further away.

For her part, Jill believes that Phyllis is a demanding and uncaring wife and that Ken and Phyllis have no real life together. She doesn't understand why it is taking Ken so long to leave Phyllis for good. She has given Ken a two-week deadline to make a decision.

Ken is an only child, with older parents. His mother was sick and increasingly confined to bed from the time Ken was seven. Ken did much of the daily caretaking of his mother in his off-school hours, and as long as he could do something to make her feel better he didn't worry too much. He suppressed any resentment at having to sacrifice his interests, and over time he learned not to pay attention to any desires that might conflict with his mother's needs. As a husband he continued along the same path, doing what Phyllis wanted and trying to make things work the way he believed they should. Over time his sacrifices have become heavy, and the long-desired rewards have not been forthcoming. Now he is torn: he wants to leave the marriage, but he can't leave without somehow taking care of Phyllis first.

Phyllis grew up in the shadow of a mother whose constant message was that Phyllis couldn't please her. Phyllis certainly tried! She takes the same approach with others, for fear of being found wanting. She has tried to "do family" as she thinks family should be done, with the goal of pleasing Ken. She is just as split as Ken between doing it right and paying attention to her own needs. Both step back from disclosing their real selves, at the same time taking refuge in the fantasy of being made whole by another.

The route for Ken and Phyllis is going to be a rough one, and their marriage may or may not survive. Both of them, however, can survive as individuals. If they are willing to learn how to pay attention to their feelings as well as to their thoughts, they can thrive as individuals, in or out of the marriage.

Are You and Your Spouse Split Selves?

As marital partners, both of you have worked hard, often for years, to build the right structure for your marriage. You've devoted yourselves to doing a good job whether it is at work, at home, in the community, or with your children. You take pride in doing things the right way, by the book. Your need to look good so as to avoid rejection leads you to tell each other "white lies." Your internal battles over whether to attend to your own needs are ones you lose. You are discouraged and depressed. Your needs remain unmet, and you don't know what to do except to keep on doing the right thing.

At the same time you see yourself as strong, priding yourself on not burdening the other spouse with unnecessary emotional details. You will handle any problem yourself. Neither of you shares your needs and feelings with the other, making it impossible to build an intimate relationship. The accommodation that initially seemed helpful has grown into a poisonous situation in which each of you manipulates the other in a manner that is superficially nice but dishonest and controlling. Deep down you withhold, refusing to risk emotionally with a spouse who is so controlling. Often, one of you has turned to the children, the other to an affair.

You were not looking for an affair but the years of not attending to your own feelings made you a prime candidate. You are charmed and excited when a friendship with a colleague begins to blossom. You have been starving emotionally—not so much by your spouse's doing as by your self-imposed emotional diet, and you leap at the feast, although not without a sense of betraying a trust. You and your colleague become seriously involved. It gets confused as you try to decide which one is the right partner for you. You don't really want to leave your spouse. Having family is very important. You certainly don't want to end the affair, although you think you should. You approach the problem rationally, "trying to make the right decision."

If you are like Ken, you probably feel upset, angry, troubled, and afraid, and you get on your own back for feeling that way.

However, an element of hope for a different future parallels your powerlessness. If you are in Phyllis's shoes you are terrified. For both of you, life as you have known it is ending, and change lies ahead. If you are in Jill's position, you are in a competition that you can lose even if you win. Each of you will need help in reclaiming and understanding the parts of your self that you sacrificed so long ago.

Exit Affairs

An Exit Affair is the vehicle for ending the marriage—not the reason. This is the kind of affair that a spouse launches when the marriage is deteriorating and it is unclear whether or how to end it. The affair provides the justification to leave. At the very least, the affair distracts the leaver from the pain in the marriage and the guilt for leaving.

Profile of Exit Affairs

- The affair is a way of sliding out the door.
- The couple's style of relating to each other is to duck difficult issues and avoid conflict.
- Body language and behavior shows that the leaver is moving away from the spouse.
- The marriage is usually of less than twelve years' duration.
- Both spouses use the affair as the reason the marriage is ending.
- Both spouses have unfinished business about loss and endings.

The Origins of Exit Affairs

Paula's Exit Affair with her old friend Brian began eight months ago. She arranged for Rob, her husband of six years, to find out by having a lengthy phone conversation with Brian when Rob was at home. When Rob picked up the phone to make a call, he ran head-first into their affair. Furious, he faced Paula the moment she was off the phone and told her what he had heard. She responded, "I was going to tell you but I didn't know how. . . . You know we haven't been getting along for a long time. . . . I don't know. I didn't want you to find out this way." Rob, even more incensed, yelled, "How long has this been going on? I thought I could trust you but you're just a cheat! You've just been using me all along! I can't believe this! I'm not going to put up with this! You better believe I'm not going to put up with this!" Paula backed away, "I don't want to talk about this now when you're so angry." Rob continued yelling until Paula left the house on the pretext of going to the grocery store.

Paula and Rob's marriage is over. It was pretty well over before Brian came on the scene. Brian was just the last nail. For Paula, getting involved with Brian validated her tentative decision to leave Rob. It will be important for Paula and Rob to understand the unfinished business that led them to end their marriage with an affair rather than talking together about the decision to close the door.

Is the Affair in Your Life an Exit Affair?

If your marriage is ending with an Exit Affair, think of the affair as the route and not the reason the marriage is ending. Choosing an affair as your escape route probably means that endings are hard for you. With an affair you can avoid facing your disappointments or talking about the unraveling of your marriage. It seems easier to let the affair carry the weight. You tell yourself that your affair partner is your one true love and that you owe it to yourself to pursue true love. You overlook your history of marital problems and give the third party total responsibility for the split.

Hopefully, the affair will get your spouse to kick you out. For that to work, your spouse will have to know about your affair. So you arrange, without quite thinking about it, to have your spouse discover your affair. Strange hotel charges on the Visa bill, lots of lengthy long-distance calls charged to your personal cellular phone, or greeting cards with mushy notes that turn up in the pocket of your shirt are common forms of evidence. Your spouse, who probably suspects already, discovers the evidence and confronts you. There is a big fight, but you are not that much involved. You are focused on getting out. If your spouse doesn't kick you out, you're disappointed. Now you will have to do something yourself in order to leave.

If you're the dumped spouse you tell yourself, "It's not anything I did; if that S.O.B. hadn't come along and played to her ego, we'd still be happily married." You are furious and you may tell your spouse to get out. If your spouse readily accepts, you may have second thoughts as she prepares to go.

It is unlikely that you will put your marriage back together. What you will need to do is understand what each of you contributed to the collapse of your marriage and why one of you chose this particularly painful way of ending your marriage. Because separating takes so much energy, you may not get to work on understanding what has happened until later.

The Third Side of the Triangle

How does the third party fit into the picture? Viewed as home wreckers or worse, third parties are actually stepping into a gap in the marriage. The third party completes someone else's triangle as a way of acting out his or her own issues. Many third parties are married, and for them the affair can be viewed in the context of their own marriage. Other third parties are single. Specific reasons that singles choose to have an affair with a married person include a fear of intimacy or of being dependent, a feeling of inner emptiness, or the pursuit of the just-out-of-reach prize. Three affair patterns are common for singles: long-term serious affairs, low-demand affairs or brief affairs such as after separating, and compulsive sex.

Profile of Singles in Long-Term Serious Affairs

- The single has been involved in the affair at least a year—probably a number of years.
- The affair partner is most likely to be a Split Self or possibly an Exiter.

- The affair represents unfinished business with parents.
- The single claims to be independent, but is really afraid of being dependent.
- The single plans personal life around the married partner's schedule and needs.

Why Singles Choose Long-Term Serious Affairs

Gwen is a never-married woman whose unfinished business with her parents set the stage for her role as third party. Gwen, who is thirty-one, has been seriously involved with Hal, fifty-two and married, for the last few years. Gwen knows that Hal loves her and intends to end his marriage to be with her, but he is staying in the marriage right now because of his kids. She's waiting for their day to come.

She may not be so happy when it does. Her relationship with Hal would become less romantic, all the little daily annoyances would intrude, and her fear of being dependent will be greater. She's been deliberately but unconsciously picking unavailable men, unknowingly trying to work out old issues. As a kid, Gwen was caught in the web of her parents' marital problems, becoming the one her father turned to when he wanted emotional support. However, she didn't have him the way she needed him: as a father who set appropriate boundaries with her and as a man who modeled a strong relationship with her mother. She also lost out with her mother, who resented Gwen's closeness with her father. She learned to give up too much of her self to men, which is why she fears being dependent, and she doesn't trust women to be fair with her.

Is Yours a Long-Term Serious Affair?

Single women, more than single men, are willing to be the third party in a long-term serious affair, usually picking an older man in a Split Self marriage. If you step into this role it is because something about your affair partner represents your unfinished business.

His romanticism coupled with his inability to make too many demands may link to your desire to be loved and cared for without becoming dependent. These affairs last for years, even until death. He plans to leave his wife, but he doesn't. When you've built your life around him, you wait it out, living a life together that parallels his life with his wife. You see his marriage as *the* obstacle to your happiness and unconsciously overlook the protection it provides against giving up too much of yourself. You think of yourself as independent, but in truth, you're afraid of being dependent.

Your work will be to understand why you're choosing to limit yourself, to examine whether you're on a track that will work for you, and to decide whether you want to make changes in your life.

Singles in Other Types of Affairs

Other affair patterns among single males and females are low-demand affairs or a series of brief affairs or one-night stands. Low-demand affairs that singles choose after separation or divorce provide attention and affection without having to make a commitment during the vulnerable period that follows separation. These affairs also incorporate an element of the testing that adolescents do to determine their attractiveness and social competence. Once you're beyond the worst of the grieving and have your feet on the ground again, you will be able to look around for someone who is unmarried and available for a more complete relationship.

Other singles choose low-demand affairs with married people because of heavy career demands or simply because they prefer a low-maintenance relationship and don't want the risks of deep emotional involvement or the obligations of commitment. Usually this pattern is tied to concerns about the cost of emotional ties or to doubts about the ability to develop a good relationship. Judy described feeling more secure with someone who is married because, "He can't abandon me, because he's not free to really be with me."

A series of one-night stands or brief affairs that is driven by the need to fill up an inner emptiness or numb inner pain means that sexual addiction is at the heart of the problem. The pattern here is much the same as the for the married Sexual Addict. However, the single Sexual Addict has fewer anchors in the world. Getting help is going to be essential to addressing your pain and changing your pattern of behavior.

Nonsexual Affairs

What about affairs that are not acted upon sexually? Are they really affairs or are they only friendships? These relationships should be considered as affairs when they consume energy that would more appropriately be going into the marriage. These relationships have a sexual current, even if sexual activity (intercourse, oral sex, fondling, kissing, and so on) is not involved. Sometimes these are affairs-in-the-making—with the affair partners moving toward physically consummating their relationship. In other cases the sexual current is sufficient for the moment.

The Internet affair is becoming a classic nonsexual affair. On the Internet, without objective data, it is easy to let one's fantasies run loose and wild, to imagine the Internet partner in idealized form—and even to present an overly idealized picture of oneself. Eric spent time every evening on the Net, chatting with Lianne. To Eric, she became a wondrous creature: sensitive, understanding, intelligent, gifted, and probably gorgeous as well. Her responses indicated that she really cared about him. Eric became determined to meet her, although he didn't know quite how he would manage that. His wife, Gayle, was already upset with the amount of time he was spending on the Net and was apprehensive about his Net relationship with Lianne.

Many Internet romances culminate in a meeting. Some turn into full-fledged affairs, others lead to shock as the fantasy crumbles in the face of reality. Internet romances, even those that remain "virtual romances," can be categorized as one of the five types of affairs, according to the underlying motivations for the affair. Eric and Gayle were Conflict Avoiders—neither of them had been talking to each other about what was bothering them. Nonsexual affairs can also be categorized according to the underlying motivations.

In many cases the marital partner overlooks the seriousness of their mate's nonsexual affair because it is nonsexual, even though a sexual undercurrent may be evident. At this point the idea of an affair can still be rationalized away. The marital partner would do well to pay attention to two common danger signals: when your spouse is spending more discretionary time with the affair partner than with you, and when your spouse's primary confidant is the affair partner and not you. If either of these patterns is present, get help now, before the nonsexual affair becomes a sexual affair. Gayle's insistence on getting marital counseling derailed Eric's plan to meet Lianne in person.

Summary

No matter how it looks to the outsider, husbands and wives don't enjoy betraying each other. They want to be loyal and trusting. When they are not, they are upset with themselves. Underlying the betrayal of the affair are the ghosts of past family problems having to do with pain, abuse, fear, abandonment and loss. This is true for third parties as well as for couples. The challenge is to identify and understand your affair pattern, and to rebuild on firmer ground, individually or as a couple. It will take time and effort and a certain amount of courage, but it is possible to resolve the problems that led to the affair. It is up to you to make a choice about whether you want to make the investment. If you decide to tackle your issues, subsequent chapters will give you guidance for doing so.

Chapter Two

The Two Sides of Telling

Will I, Won't I . . . /
Do I Want to Know?

Secrets lead to pain whether you hide them, lie
about them, or reveal them. What paths will the
pain take?

Carol and Mark aren't in crisis yet. But the stage has been set by
Carol's affair. She dreads the day that Mark discovers it, but she
yearns for relief from her burden of secrecy. "Will telling mean I
have to give up Kevin? I don't know if I can do that. Mark might
just decide to walk out. Maybe if I apologize and beg him to forgive
me and promise it will never happen again it will blow over before
too long. But I don't know—I don't think he's going to be very forgiving. I don't know what to do!"

Russ is less ambivalent. "What? Tell my wife? I can't do that!
She'd never forgive me! Besides, there's no point in hurting her. I'll
just end it and we'll work out our problems and she'll never know."

We get mixed messages about keeping secrets. Many people
live by the old maxim, "What you don't know won't hurt you."
Some warn, "Telling a person something that's going to hurt them
is just plain cruel." Others insist, "Honesty is always the best policy." Your ideas about what to do with your secret will be colored by
your beliefs and fears and family patterns.

All affairs begin in secret. But then what? Guilt, fear, hope, and
happenstance play a role in whether an affair is revealed. With
some couples, the affair surfaces relatively soon. Other affairs are
hidden for months or years. Sometimes the affair surfaces only to
be explained away and denied.

If you're having an affair, the big question for you is whether you're going to reveal this secret to your partner, and if so, how. Your options are to tell your partner, to get someone else to fill your partner in, to set up your partner to discover your affair, or to do nothing and hope for the best.

Lying and dishonesty stem from a desire to protect yourself and to minimize the payments for any risks you take. That doesn't mean you don't take risks—just the opposite. You worry about paying for the risks you have taken and try to shift the payment elsewhere, or you may deny that there's a cost. As long as the affair is hidden, the idea is that nothing changes. But everything changes. Nothing flows quite so smoothly. Little things, little inconsistencies arise and are explained away if confronted.

If you're the betrayed spouse, you buy in, wanting to believe, wanting your marriage to be the marriage you think it is, wanting your partner to be the person you think he is. But long blond hairs, echoes of a different scent, phone bills with strange numbers, and the like keep floating to the surface. They float away again as you look away, trying to explain to yourself in rational terms how this could be and how at the same time your spouse is who you think he is. Distance develops as each of you dances, neither telling the truth, both now into self-protection.

The secret affair is akin to the emperor who wore no clothes: everyone in the family and many of those outside know something is going on but no one is talking. As the secret grows it begins to take on a life of its own. It is not just the affair that is hidden, but other lies are told and other secrets kept. More and more topics of conversation are taboo. In the background is the threat that your spouse may discover your affair anyway. Most likely your partner suspects but isn't ready—yet—to have those suspicions confirmed.

Some people decide to tell their partner themselves. Others, unconsciously on purpose, decide to inform their spouse in other ways. Certain patterns of revealing the secret are typical with different types of affairs. An Exiter can't use an affair as the reason to leave the marriage if it's still hidden. Exiters are famous for "accidentally" leaving clues lying around for their partner to stumble over. Intimacy Avoiders usually let each other know early about affairs—affairs are perfect weapons for continuing to fight, thereby avoiding intimacy. Sexual Addicts don't really hide their behavior; they just deny it is a problem. Although the Sexual Addict's affairs are revealed time after time, the betrayed partner hides this secret from outsiders. Conflict Avoiders and Split Selves are likely to hang on to the secret of the affair longer than anyone else because they so fear conflict and the consequences of telling.

The next section speaks to the suspicious spouse about recognizing the signs of an affair and confronting the partner. The following section guides the betraying spouse in exploring the consequences of revealing or of not revealing the affair to the spouse.

When You Think Your Partner Is Having an Affair

Worried that your partner might be having an affair? Your suspicions may be right on target. Usually you know, consciously or unconsciously, when your partner is having an affair. When you are not ready to know, you explain away your unanswered questions and stifle your uneasiness. Eventually it's time to know. Sometimes you're ready to know before your spouse is ready to tell.

Recognizing the Signs and Signals of an Affair

The kinds of changes that signal an affair tend to start without warning. Suddenly your spouse starts criticizing you, your sex life changes, a friend's name suddenly drops into the conversation or drops out, your spouse's physical appearance suddenly spiffs up, or your spouse becomes moody and unavailable. Secrets are "crazy-making," and you feel more and more confused. You know down deep that your marriage is off track but you can't account for it, and you scramble around trying to make things right without knowing what is wrong. You doubt your perceptions and your self. You look for clues that will reveal what's going on but you are so confused that you explain away the evidence you see. Later on, when you— a short-haired blonde—ask your husband about the long black hairs on his undershirt, he explains that he must have picked them up when he was working out. You try to believe him because anything else is inconceivable. Anything else means that life as you've known it is over.

It's likely that your spouse has been handing you some clues. Most people having an affair are troubled enough by carrying the secret that they unconsciously arrange for you to stumble across evidence of it. Sometimes the signs are displayed in living color in front of your eyes, but you choose to turn away for now. The particulars often show up on long-distance phone bills or charge accounts. They surface in personal notes, strange hair combs, sudden criticism that doesn't make sense. Sometimes the third party tells you of the affair, hoping to provoke you into ending the marriage and leaving the field clear. Chance events often converge to uncover the secret, as when the florist tucks the note for the third party into your Valentine bouquet.

Somewhere in this period you may decide to get marriage counseling. This can be helpful provided the truth comes out. Your partner may ask the counselor for help in telling you of the affair, or the counselor may suspect an affair and work toward getting it out in the open. Occasionally the affair is so well hidden that the counselor is unaware of it. If your partner tells the counselor of the affair but won't tell you, many marriage counselors will refuse to see you for marital counseling. Most counselors believe that a secret this big sitting silently in the room makes honest communication with your partner impossible. Some counselors, however, will collude in keeping the secret. If couples' counseling doesn't work, individual counseling can be useful in helping you decide on your next steps.

When you are ready for the truth, it is time to confront your spouse. One woman spoke of her fear about learning the truth, "If you don't know for sure that you can live with it, then you don't want to know." You're ready to know when the craziness of living with the secret becomes overwhelming; when knowing the truth about your marriage, no matter how painful, is more important to you than ducking your pain and fear. Researchers haven't tabulated the long-term results of disclosing affairs, but they have found with other issues that it's not the bad news, "It's the lack of knowledge that tends to make people miserable."[1]

How to Confront Your Spouse

If you have reason to suspect an affair but don't have hard evidence, tell your spouse what you think, in a short simple statement, and wait for an answer. It is harder for the person having the affair to lie in response to "I think you're having an affair," than to "Are you having an affair?" The latter question only asks for a yes or no. "I think you're having an affair" demands a more detailed response. Phrase and voice your statement in a calm way so that your partner isn't reacting to your style but to your message. Make your statement, then stay silent and wait for your spouse to respond. Don't clutter up this confrontation with a big preamble or postscript. Otherwise you give your spouse time to come up with a "good answer," and you'll miss your spouse's initial reactions.

Observe the verbal and nonverbal responses. Is there an embarrassed silence? Is there a fumbling denial or a beating around the bush? Are there questions that put you on the defensive, such as "What makes you say that?" Don't sidetrack your confrontation by taking the bait; wait for a response—or a nonresponse. In that way you will have your answer.

One Saturday afternoon, when the kids were at the movies with friends, Judy sat Russ down and said to him, "Russ, I know something's going on and I think you're having an affair." Russ was slow to answer. Finally he said, "What gives you that idea?" Judy responded, "I just think so," and she waited. Russ shifted in his seat, then mumbled something about, "Well, it's not really an affair; I mean I haven't seen her very often." Judy looked him in the eye and said, "Don't lie to me! You're admitting you're involved in an affair, but now you're telling me it's not really an affair. Get real!" Russ acknowledged, "Well, I guess it is an affair. But I didn't want to hurt you."

If your spouse is not involved in an affair, the response will be a simple, believable no, followed by a straightforward, low-key discussion. Any other response is a yes. If your spouse owns up, you will feel shock edged with relief, to be followed by pain and fury. If there is no owning up—and your jealousy is not working overtime—your spouse is too scared or too confused or too arrogant to admit the affair, or there is another big secret but it's not an affair.

You may be considering using a private investigator. Be careful! To do so adds another triangle to the original one and it's rare that "getting the goods" buys you anything of value. Instead, it heightens the intrigue, the excitement, and the retaliation factor. Adding the investigator as another third party in the situation can result in a rapid escalation of conflict, leading toward litigation and reducing chances of working out your marital problems. The more people involved in your personal situation, the harder it will be for the two of you to decide what's best for you.

It is more useful for you to learn to pay attention to your deeper feelings and to trust them. You know when things are not going well. You know when information is missing. You know when there is a secret. You may not want to know, but you know when things are off. One study found that 89 percent of spouses knew at some level that their partners were having an affair.[2] Trust your knowledge that there is a secret. Usually it's an affair. In the few instances when the secret is not an affair, it is a secret with relevance for your marriage, such as a large financial gift made to a relative without your knowledge.

When your marriage feels off track, these are steps you can take:

- Pay attention to your feelings that something is wrong. Judy admitted, "I knew something—for months I was feeling scared."

- Assess whether your discomfort stems from your own insecurities or from real changes in your partner's behavior.
- Confront your partner by making a statement about what you think, as in "I think you're having an affair"—not "You're cheating on me."
- Listen to what your partner has to say, and observe your partner's response.
- Be prepared for your own emotional reaction when you are face to face with the secret.

When You Are the One Having an Affair

If your affair is still a secret, you probably are very ambivalent about revealing it to your spouse. You feel guilty, your stomach hurts, you're afraid your spouse will find out—and you're afraid she won't. Then you'll have to feel miserable forever—better to have her find out and get it over with. But no—she might leave and she'd take the kids with her too. Some days you try to tune out all those nagging thoughts and feelings. You reassure yourself rationally, "Everyone does it. And if she doesn't know she won't be hurt. In fact, nobody's getting hurt. It's just not a big thing! I'll end it and that will be that. But I don't know if I can end it!" On other days you go back and forth between worrying and tuning out.

Meanwhile you invent excuses for coming home late, for not answering the phone when you're "working late," for your preoccupation. You judge your spouse's inadequacies as a way of justifying your behavior. Pretty soon your spouse notices changes and asks if you're having an affair. You lie again, and sometimes you even accuse your spouse of being crazy to think such a thing. For a while your spouse buys in, not wanting to believe there's an affair. Both of you fear disclosure.

There is no easy or pleasant way out. Will you decide to reveal the secret or will you let things take their course, hoping that your secret stays buried? Or have you unconsciously arranged for your spouse to discover the evidence? If not, you will need to resolve your ambivalence so that you can tell your partner about your affair. Only then can the two of you begin to examine the issues you've both been avoiding. If you don't tell, it may take hours, weeks, or years, but eventually a puzzle piece falls into place, and the affair rises out of the dark and into the spotlight.

To tell or not to tell! Whatever your decision, it will have major consequences. At some level, you know it's too big a secret to keep. You don't have many options—and none of your options are painless. Some options carry hope for the long run. Others leave you with a potentially explosive secret. None comes with any guarantees. There is no comfortable way out—only painful options, each with its own risk.

There are few really big decisions in life, but this is one of them. It's important to make your decision carefully. Right now you're probably leaning toward not telling. You hope that if you don't tell, nobody will be the wiser and things can go along as they are—forgetting for the moment that one of the reasons behind the affair is that things are not so great the way they are. On the other hand, keeping this secret has been taking a terrible toll on you.

Cautions

Being afraid to tell your spouse about your affair and imagining all sorts of dire outcomes is natural. When you feel guilty, your imagination can build wondrous nightmares. You see yourself cowering in the wake of your spouse's fury. You picture your spouse screaming at you or crying or hitting you. You might even want to hit back. Or maybe your spouse will run out the door with your kids, never to return, or you'll be sent packing with only the clothes on your back. You know you can't fix it right now—besides, you don't know how. You wonder if you'll be in the doghouse forever. These are normal fears, but in most cases they're exaggerated. There are situations, however, that require consideration and caution.

If your spouse has a history of physical violence or if you have been physically afraid of your spouse in the past, issues of physical safety need to be addressed before you tell. Using your past experience, assess whether your spouse will react to the disclosure of your affair with *physical* violence. Being furious and yelling is not physical violence. Hitting and kicking is. So is using a knife or a gun.

Sometimes an affair triggers a deep rage that wells up from early emotional wounds that have festered, although the person has never before been physically violent. When the potential for physical violence is present, violence related to your affair may erupt even if you don't come clean. Your spouse may suspect the truth or learn of it from other sources. Other factors such as *severe* mental illness, alcoholism, or suppressed and simmering rage also indicate a need for caution. Don't underestimate the need to assess your safety. When such a risk is present, get professional help immediately to sort out your next steps, including whether to tell. (And read Chapter Four, which discusses the problem of violence in more detail.)

Is yours an Exit Affair? You may be afraid that adultery charges will result if you are honest about your affair. These days, charges of adultery seldom have much impact in court. Despite a long history of serving up punishment for adultery, most divorce courts just don't care any more, and decisions about money, property, and kids are generally based on different criteria. However some courts still do care, particularly in certain parts of the United States and in rural areas, or when the judge's personal experience bleeds into judicial decisions. You need to know the situation in your state and your community. Also, some betrayed spouses, intentionally or not, seek an attorney with a reputation for making the errant partner pay for the betrayal, even if it bankrupts you both.

Occasionally a person remains in the marriage to care for a spouse who is permanently and significantly incapacitated, and tries to make a life with another partner on the side. If you are staying in the marriage to care for a partner who is bedridden, for example, disclosing your affair might relieve your guilt, but will it be helpful for your marriage or your spouse? In deciding whether to tell it's important to look at that question.

Deciding Whether or Not to Tell

For most of you the cautions just described won't apply. That means it's time to face the issue of whether you are going to reveal your affair to your spouse or not. Only with honesty can you rebuild your marriage on more solid ground. You can't build intimacy on a base of betrayal and dishonesty—intimacy requires having everything out on the table. That's why honesty is so important.

You will need to decide for yourself whether you believe honesty affects intimacy. If you do, and you want an intimate relationship, your next decision is whether to tell your spouse of your affair. Honesty comes with risks, however. Revealing your affair exposes everything, even your hiding places. Once the affair is out, you will have to deal with the larger picture or find a way to stuff it under the rug. Dealing with the affair isn't a guarantee that your marriage will survive. Thus you need to be clear with yourself in making this pivotal decision.

The Four Square Analysis is an effective tool for teasing apart all the likely consequences of your decision. You can use this framework to outline your thoughts and feelings, your fears and your hopes, as you answer the following questions.

1. What do you think the best possible outcome will be if you don't tell your spouse about your affair?
2. What is the worst possible outcome if you don't tell?
3. What is the best possible outcome if you reveal your affair to your spouse?
4. What is the worst possible outcome of telling?

Carol's first pass using this process is typical:

	Tell	**Don't Tell**
Best	Mark will forgive her and they can start over	The status quo
Worst	The marriage will end	Nothing will change

Carol's second look has more depth:

	Tell	**Don't Tell**
Best	Might face and resolve problems Would like each other again Develop a stronger connection Marriage counseling helps	Status quo tolerable for now Buy some time and see what happens
Worst	The marriage ends and it's ugly Stay married but Mark doesn't let it go Mark gets custody of the kids	Mark finds out anyway and is so angry he starts legal battle and it's even uglier I'd always feel guilty

Go through this process several times, going deeper each time. Include what would happen if your spouse finds out anyway. Probably most of your reasons for not telling come down to being afraid to face the consequences of your involvement in an affair. After you have done this, repeat the process, this time filling in more details about the likely outcomes. Envision how each possible scenario plays out a year from now, and what each looks like in five years. Then read what you have written and use it to begin moving toward a decision. Rule out those options you cannot live with, and consider all the others. You may also want to read the next section on how to tell your spouse about your affair before you reach a decision. You can go through this exercise as many times as you need.

After you have a detailed picture of all the possible outcomes, consider where your best chances lie, and decide where you are going to put your cards. For example, Carol's sense of things on her third time through is different yet:

	Tell	Don't Tell
Best	Intimacy depends on honesty—we build some intimacy There are risks both ways—this at least has positive potential	We keep going along A miracle happens
Worst	Our marriage ends, and it's a mess I can't forgive myself Mark finds out, loses all trust, kids get caught in middle I might have another affair	Our communication would get worse It would be a charade, I'd be living a lie

Carol wants an intimate marriage with Mark. She's never wanted the marriage to end. She decides that her best hope is in being honest. "I guess I made the decision back when I got involved. If I hadn't done that, I wouldn't have anything to tell. Now it's settle-up time. And it scares the hell out of me!"

You don't have to understand how the affair happened to be ready to tell. Sorting it out comes after telling. Nor does the affair have to be over before you tell your partner. By revealing your affair you start down a path of dealing more honestly with your spouse and yourself. If you still cannot decide what to do, you might want someone to help you think this issue through. Choose someone who is accepting and not judgmental, a person who will help you come to your own decision rather than make your decision for you. Professional help is often the best choice (see Chapter Nine). Most marital therapists believe that if you want a close and intimate relationship with your spouse, honesty about your affair is required. Not all the experts agree—a few believe that you can successfully hide an affair without unduly affecting the marriage.

If you decide not to tell, keep tabs on the impact that this decision is having on you and your marriage. Do you find yourself having to lie to cover up old lies? Do you feel more distant from your spouse, or does there seem to be more tension between the two of you? How are your kids reacting to the tension? Do guilt feelings nag at you periodically? A month from now, if things are not genuinely better (not just buried deeper), take the time to reexamine your decision.

Planning to Tell

Telling your spouse about your affair is one of the hardest things you will ever do. What do you say? And how do you say it? And when? Is there any good way to do this? *How you tell* your partner of your affair is crucial. The most essential element is that you take responsibility for your behavior without blaming your spouse. Be gentle—your spouse has enough of a bombshell to deal with. If you've had more than one affair, get the whole picture out in the open. Dribbling additional secrets out over time raises even more questions about whether your word is reliable.

Telling is hard, hard, hard. You'll consider putting it off, yet getting it over with has a certain appeal. You will be tempted to minimize or misrepresent the situation in hopes of making it easier on everyone. It won't work. If you distort, as in saying it was a short affair when it was really eight months, the burden of your secrets will still be with you. When your attempts to minimize are unsuccessful, your spouse will be even angrier at your continuing deception.

How you see yourself and your behavior is part of what makes telling so hard. How have you been thinking of yourself? As a rat? A sneak? A sleaze? Are you feeling ashamed? Now's your chance to change those adjectives. How do you want to think of yourself?

Can you disclose your affair in a way that makes you feel more responsible? You won't get any brownie points right now from anyone but yourself, but for you it's a step toward your own integrity. Consider it another one of those "growth experiences."

If you're going to tell, make it simple and clear. Leave out all the extra words that you're tempted to put in when you're anxious. A big apologetic preamble just raises your spouse's anxiety about what awful truth is coming. Omit the "I'm sorry"s, the "I don't want to hurt you"s, and the "Please forgive me"s. Although designed to soften your spouse's reaction, they will do just the opposite. Saying you're sorry before you even provide the facts comes across as "It's OK, it's over, I've told you and I've said I'm sorry, so now you can just forget about it." That's what we learned as kids: say "I'm sorry" and it's all over. Your spouse won't see it like that. She will be enraged by this attempt to control her reaction. Especially forget, "I love you honey. . . . I had an affair," which is guaranteed to inflame her.

Give the tough information first without trying to fix the situation. Mumbling "I've sort of been involved with someone," isn't clear and it forces your spouse to guess or to grill you. The kindest way to tell is to say only, "I need to tell you something: I'm having an affair."

Another tempting trap is to say, "My therapist convinced me to tell you." This too, will infuriate your partner—after hiding your affair, you are hiding behind the therapist. Translation: "I didn't want to be honest with you," or "It's the therapist's fault I'm hurting you." If you have the courage to tell, own your decision. It is a major and positive step for you to decide to be honest about your behavior.

You can use this checklist as you make your final preparations to tell:

- Practice saying out loud whatever you decide to say, so that you hear your own words and can tolerate saying them without decoration or dissembling.

- Decide when you will disclose your secret. Choose a time when you will be available to your spouse—and when neither of you is about to leave for work, go out of town, or otherwise disappear. No hit and run!

- Remember to "own" your behavior. Don't blame your affair on your spouse.

- Expect to feel scared, but don't let your fear take over.

- Be as ready as you can be for your spouse's response: shock, pain, anger, questions, or a combination of these.

- Know that you will need to listen to your spouse's reaction, no matter what the response is. Resist the temptation to apologize so as to soften your spouse's reaction—it won't work.

- If you are in therapy, ask for your therapist's help in preparing to tell your spouse and consider whether to disclose your affair in a couple's session or at home.

Telling

There are better times to tell, and worse times, but there's never a good time. When your plans are made, it's time to tell. Carol decided to tell Mark on a Thursday after the kids were in bed. That way they had Thursday night to talk, the buffer of work on Friday, and the weekend when they could talk or could get some distance from each other. Their discussion is typical of many couples: Carol starts out well, but when Mark gets angry she gets scared and begins apologizing. Her apologies make Mark even angrier. Her other responses to Mark don't escalate his anger.

> *Carol:* Mark, there's something I need to tell you. It's very
>   important.
> *Mark:* Ummm?
> *Carol:* I've been having an affair.
> *Mark:* (*speechless, then furious*) I knew something was wrong!

How could you? It's with Kevin, isn't it? You've been lying to me all along! I thought you and Kevin had something going on but you always acted like I was being ridiculous. Well I'm not ridiculous! No wife of mine is going to make me look ridiculous. I'm not going to put up with it! How about that?!

Carol: I'm sorry, I didn't want to hurt you—

Mark: Sorry! Sorry! You don't know what sorry means!

Carol: Mark, I feel awful. I know I shouldn't have done it. I didn't mean to hurt you—I uh, I don't know why I did it. I don't want our marriage to end.

Mark: So how long has this been going on?

Carol: For about five months. I ended it last week.

Mark: Why should I believe that?

Carol: I don't know—

Mark: (*pacing*) I really don't want to believe any of this! I can't believe this is happening.

Carol: It's true. I hate seeing you so upset. What can I do to make you feel better?

Mark: Nothing! Just leave me alone right now! (*Mark retreats so that he can take in what he's just heard. Carol cleans up the kitchen and goes to bed. Mark comes in and they exchange a few words. Neither sleeps very well.*)

When the moment comes and you know you are about to tell, take a deep breath and say what you've decided to say. In telling, keep the following points in mind:

- Be gentle—spare the hurtful details.
- Be available to your spouse while he or she absorbs the shock.
- Let your spouse know that you feel bad about the pain you have caused.
- When your spouse asks, be ready to tell your spouse who the affair is with, how long it has lasted, whether it has ended, and who else knows about it.

- Don't ask to be forgiven now.
- Let your spouse know if you want to work on the marriage.

When the Affair Is Disclosed

No matter how prepared you are, disclosure of an affair is traumatic. Life changes for both of you, and there's no place to hide. *Now is the time for emotions, not action.* You need to take in the enormity of what has happened to your marriage and your selves before you make any decisions or take any actions. Just taking it in is plenty for now.

After Learning You've Been Betrayed

If you're the one who's been betrayed, your heart doesn't want to believe what your head knows is the truth. You may want to isolate yourself or curl up in a fetal ball. This state of shock may last minutes, or hours, or days. Then your pain takes over and you cry. You fight against it by asking why, why, why and by blaming and obsessing about the affair. You have your angry moments too, but those get you too close to your pain so you go back to your questions. You're afraid of what will happen next. Will your marriage survive? Will you survive?

Even though you're increasingly furious, ignore the advice of friends and relatives to rush to the nearest divorce attorney. *Legal proceedings don't resolve emotional issues. Take time for your pain and your anger before taking action of any sort.* See if you can keep your focus on your own pain and anger rather than on attacking your spouse. And whatever you do, leave your children out of it for now. There is time enough later for deciding how to talk with the children about the turmoil in the family. Right now you both need time to absorb the impact of this disclosure.

Forget the temptation to separate immediately. Going home to visit mother for a few weeks so you don't have to deal with the situation or telling your spouse to leave will not help. Fleeing gives the illusion that you can avoid your pain, but the pain goes with you. Separate bedrooms in the same house are OK for the moment—each of you may need some space when you feel so raw and vulnerable—just don't separate. Better to sit tight and see how the two of you got to this point before making any decisions.

"I can't trust you" is a common theme. Of course you can't! Right now neither of you can trust each other: you don't understand why this has happened and you haven't gone through a period of rebuilding your relationship. You're faced with giving up your ideal of a spouse who would never hurt you. Judy declared, "I was absolutely sure that Russ would never, never do that to me! I still can't believe it. But he did it!"

Judy needs to express her pain and Russ needs to hear it, right now when it's raw. If your situation resembles that of Russ and Judy, your spouse will probably want to appease you so that he or she doesn't have to be a witness to your pain. Resist any attempts by your spouse to get you to "be nice" or to dismiss or suppress your pain and your anger. Don't let your voice be shut off, especially by a quick "I love you" or a guilty "I'm sorry." Neither love nor guilt makes it OK. If your partner offers a lame excuse, such as, "She came after me, and I didn't know what to do," don't trap yourself into believing him just because you "want it to be over." Blaming the third party won't work either—it's your spouse who betrayed you.

Expect the intensity of your pain to be as strong as your anger. When Judy was finally able to put her experience into words, she said, "I was so devastated, I wanted to lay down and die." Stay with what you *feel*, even when it's as painful as it was for Judy. Don't get sidetracked into analyzing or making premature decisions. Trying to make decisions you're not ready to make won't end your pain, and some of those decisions might even make things worse for you. It's not the time to make big decisions. It will be over when it's over. You've got lots to do between now and then.

What will help right now is someone who cares that you hurt; who is there so you don't have to be alone with your pain.

Hopefully this will be your spouse. Being with you and hearing your pain is a major step for the betraying spouse. However, if your partner just can't deal with your pain, or if your spouse has decided to leave, you need the comfort of someone who does care about you. Or it may be that you're not ready yet to share your pain with your spouse. Confide in a trusted friend or relative who cares about you both and will not take sides. Choose someone who will support you but won't let you settle for playing victim, who won't drive any additional wedges between you and your spouse, and who doesn't give advice.

Despite the pain, knowing the truth is freeing, and it enables you to take back your power. You're no longer in that crazy phase where nothing makes sense.

After Your Affair Is Disclosed

When you're the one who had the affair, telling your partner provides some relief but you can expect to feel guilt and pain at the anguish you have caused, and helpless in the wake of your spouse's emotions. You too wonder about survival.

At first, let your partner's response be a guide. Some spouses have questions immediately; others are in shock and want some space alone. Your partner will have plenty of questions once the shock wears off. Be prepared to answer them, telling who the third party is, whether the affair is still going on, and how long it has lasted. You may protest the idea of disclosing the identity of the third party, but your spouse will interpret your protection of the third party as another slap in the face. Provide an honest picture of the total situation, such as whether this affair occurred on "marital turf" (say, your home or your favorite restaurant), and whether there have been other affairs. Give your partner the information you would want if your situations were reversed. Mark asked, "Am I the laughing stock of the whole town?" Carol reassured Mark that she hadn't told their families or their couple friends of her affair, although she had told her best friend.

With the affair out in the open, the pain is evident, present in every look and word. The issue is too big to be fixed right now so don't get into fixing. You're probably feeling horrible about the pain you've caused your spouse. Let it show—it says you care. Resist the desire to say, "Don't get upset." Your spouse has the right to feel upset. She won't be able to accept comfort from you now, but she will want to talk with you about your betrayal, if not now, in the immediate future. Reassure her that you will be available to talk and to listen, that you're not going to disappear.

You won't resolve anything right now, but abandoning your spouse after unloading the secret is like putting fire to oil. If there's even a chance you want this marriage, you need to embrace your spouse's anguish. This is the start of mutual efforts to get everything on the table—something that's new for both of you. Alternatively, if your spouse wants time alone, honor that request, making yourself available when your spouse is ready for comfort or communication.

Getting Practical Help

Consider too, getting help from a couples therapist for the two of you together. Individual therapy at this time can be counterproductive because it allows you to continue avoiding each other—and that is a major part of how you got to this point. However, if your spouse won't go with you for help, go by yourself.

If the affair is an Exit Affair, you will probably need help in the near future with practical matters; maybe from a mediator or an attorney (see Chapter Nine). With other types of affairs you don't need this help immediately. In fact, seeing an attorney instantly often escalates the conflict between the two of you, reduces any possibility of working on the marriage, and delays your emotional work. Keep your eye right now on your emotional work. A counselor can help you with that. Maybe you'll never need a mediator or an attorney.

Summary

With the affair out in the open, you can begin exploring where you are and what it means. Choose carefully how you move ahead. You have a major opportunity for which you've each paid dearly. Don't waste it on a dead-end route such as selling your dream house, moving to the ideal community, losing weight, or just shoving the affair under the rug and going on as if nothing has happened. A change of symbols doesn't resolve the problem, and the space under the rug is bursting at the seams. Instead, consider the affair an invitation to think about needed changes. It is an opportunity not to be wasted, or as one woman said, "It's another one of those growth experiences I'd rather do without!" The next chapter will help you get started. It is intended as first aid to get you safely through the heart-wrenching first days after the affair is revealed.

Chapter Three

Facing the Affair

Pathways offering you choices are found in
between fighting and fleeing.

"I can't believe this is happening, please, someone, tell me this is all a bad dream!" cries Kim. Jason pleads, "I'm sorry. You know I really didn't mean to hurt you. I don't know what else to say." Kim retorts, "If you didn't want to hurt me then why did you get involved with that woman?! Did she come after you?" Jason looks away, "I don't really know." Kim fires back, "What do you mean, you don't know!" By the twenty-third time they've gone through this confrontation, they're angry, exhausted, and stuck.

With the affair out in the open, the emotions of both partners are all over the place. An affair in your life seems beyond belief. Except you know it's real. And neither of you has any idea what to do next. The possibilities that cross your mind, like strangling your spouse or walking out, have a certain appeal, but they aren't very practical. It may be hard to imagine, but other possibilities exist for both of you.

Yes, it is possible to survive an affair, even if you don't believe it right now. But we're going to talk about more than just survival. Recovering from an affair, your own or your partner's, is about grieving and growing and coming out the better for it. You can choose to plant your feet and fight, withdraw in flight, or face the opportunity for needed but difficult change. Since you're already feeling miserable, you might as well stick around and get the benefits of facing your situation. One day you'll be able to say, like Mark, whose wife had an affair after eight years of marriage, "I would never have believed that we'd come out of this OK. If the affair hadn't shaken us both up our marriage would be dead by now. It was definitely headed for burial." Or maybe you'll be more like Ron, who left his wife through an affair: "I feel very badly about the way I left my marriage, but we've both done a lot of growing since, and I think we'll end up being better friends now than we were as husband and wife."

This is the time to slow down and move cautiously. *Your future depends on how you handle this crisis.*

Avoiding Common Traps

To come out of this whole, you both need to consider carefully your next steps and refrain from acting impulsively or pursuing revenge. Take the time you need to do so.

Traps lie at every intersection. You may be trying so hard to avoid the traps that you don't see where hope and opportunities lie, much like walking along a rutted road watching where you walk but missing the gorgeous wildflowers just a few feet from you. Traps that lie in wait for both of you along your rutted road include the following:

- Disclosing only a part of the picture
- Trying to make the big decisions right now when you're in crisis
- Looking for a rational explanation to solve an emotional problem
- Seeing divorce as the only answer
- Looking for people to take your side
- Trying to outrun your pain and your fear
- Not seeing or using the positive opportunities presented by this crisis
- Trying to move on without taking the time you need

Additional traps that can snare the betrayed partner include:

- Focusing on the third party
- Continuing to obsess about the affair

- Engaging in revenge or retaliation
- Forgiving prematurely

Each of these traps presents a choice. You can let yourself fall into the trap, or you can choose a different route. Some of the possibilities for you to consider follow.

Disclose the Full Picture

It's so tempting to reveal only part of the picture. You hope that by minimizing or leaving out certain information the negative consequences will be reduced. Usually, it's just the opposite. Eventually, the truth comes to light. The continuing dishonesty results in making the consequences worse than they otherwise would have been. Mark wearily confronted his wife, "You lied to me about the affair. Then after I pushed you on it, you admitted to it. You said you'd told me everything. And now I find out you haven't told me everything at all. You lied when you said it was over. And you lied about how long it's gone on. And I don't know what else you've been lying about, all the time telling me that I can trust you. I'd just started thinking we might be able to work this out, but you're just a liar and a cheat and I don't want to have anything to do with you."

Partial honesty won't get you any credit. The full picture must be disclosed or subsequent efforts to work on the relationship will be undermined by the remaining secrets.

Delay Big Decisions Right Now

By the time an affair has occurred, there's a tangled web underneath the surface of your marriage that is not easily understood. Revealing the affair is the first step toward resolution, but it's a scary and stormy step. With disclosure, things come to a head, and you're in crisis. The first rule is to make no major decisions when you're in the midst of a crisis. Slowing down and getting beneath the surface will improve your ability to make better decisions at a later time.

Look at the Emotional Issues

Facing an affair is one of the hardest things you will ever do, whether it is your own affair or your partner's. An affair tells you that something has gotten way off track in your emotional life. You'll look for rational reasons that explain it all—quickly—in hopes that you can fix it fast and make the pain go away. However, affairs don't happen for rational reasons. They happen for emotional reasons, and emotional issues take time to understand. Pain and guilt are as much a part of the picture as love and lust—usually more so. It's easy to get stuck trying to understand. For now, pay attention to what you're *feeling* in this moment—not what you're feeling about the affair, your marriage, or your partner, but simply what you're feeling inside.

Don't Assume Divorce

At times, divorce seems like the only answer. It's not. It's not even the most common result of an affair. However, you probably have friends and relatives telling you, "I wouldn't put up with it if my wife had an affair," or "Husbands that cheat deserve to be thrown out," and urging you to go see their divorce attorney. An affair doesn't automatically mean divorce. Moreover, divorce may not be the right solution for you. You have a variety of choices, and you owe it to yourself to take plenty of time to check them out so that you can pick a solution that fits you.

Get Support from Friends

You're going to need emotional support to get through this. True support comes in the form of listening, providing comfort, and keeping your confidences. It can mean giving you information you've asked for. It does not include giving you advice, bad-mouthing your spouse, or taking your side.

Beware of unsolicited advice you get from some of your best friends and your well-meaning relatives. They want to help you with your pain and they want to see you express your anger. They may also want to vicariously avenge a few wrongs in their own life. Even though they love you, they are probably caught up in the drama, and they too have learned crazy ideas about affairs, so they don't really know how to help. They may believe that they have to take sides. You're better off if they don't.

Pay Attention to Your Pain and Your Fear

Whether you've been betrayed or done the betraying, you are probably feeling powerless and exhausted. When you're not furious you're tempted to bury the problems still deeper. You'll need to do something else with your emotions to put yourself on the road to recovery.

Whatever steps you take right now, you're going to feel a lot of pain, so there's no point in trying to outrun it. Plan on sitting tight for the moment and paying attention to whatever you feel: hurt, guilty, helpless, hopeless, or fearful. If you're angry, look underneath the anger to find your deeper emotions. You don't need to act on any of these feelings and you probably shouldn't. You do need to let yourself feel them and grieve. Your feelings, working along with your rational self, will help guide you as you move ahead. It's the feelings that you don't pay attention to that can push you in directions you don't want to go.

Use This Crisis as an Opportunity

It is ironic that an affair, intended to avoid pain of one sort or another, creates more pain. As with most growth, it is your pain that provides the motivation for change—that lets you know that the nagging issues that you have avoided can no longer be ignored. Your challenge is to use the opportunity provided by the affair and not let it go to waste. Using the opportunity means learning to talk straight to yourself and to your partner. It means learning how to negotiate to get your needs met. It means taking your own pain seriously and treating your dreams, hopes, fears, and pain with reverence and respect. It means learning to hear your partner's pain without trying to cover it up or provide a quick fix. Remember that affairs are a problem that *can* be dealt with.

Take the Time You Need

With the affair out in the open, you're devastated and you feel as if your world is coming apart. Both of you will need to give up the idea of quick solutions—*there is no quick solution.* The only thing that's quick is to run away, and the price for that is high. Putting your life back together, together or individually, takes time. As you resolve your issues you will have a clearer idea of whether your marriage can be saved—and whether you want to save it.

Focus on Your Relationship, Not the Third Party

A big danger is assuming the affair or the third party is the problem and continuing to ignore the buried issues that are eating away at you and your marriage. The third party is not the issue; the affair is not even the issue. Problems in your relationship are the issue. The third party can provide an escape for each of you from issues you're afraid to tackle. As long as you focus your anger and guilt on the third party, that person will continue to influence your marriage, whether in reality or in spirit. Your energy will be better spent on problem solving and rebuilding.

Shift from Obsessing About the Affair to Experiencing Where You Are Now

Obsessing about the affair and the third party allows you to avoid feeling your emotions at a time when you are raw. Obsessing is thinking about the past, going over and over what has happened, trying to make rational sense of it. Irv is obsessing when he protests to his wife Eileen for the umpteenth time, "You just don't do this to your husband! And if I didn't know about this, what else don't I know about? You need to tell me all the details. Is he better in bed? What's he got that I don't? Did he proposition you? What did he say? How could you do this?" And on and on and on. Irv is not saying anything about what's going on inside himself emotionally, and he's alienating Eileen.

If you're like Irv you need to shift gears. Ask yourself, "What am I feeling this very moment?" If you don't know what you're feeling, explore how your body is reacting. Are your muscles tight? Is your stomach upset? Do you have a headache? See if you can tell what your body is telling you about what you feel. Your feelings, as difficult as they are, need your attention.

Resist Your Desire for Revenge or Retaliation

Affairs are so painful, the highs and lows so extreme, that the temptation to squander your rage on retaliation and revenge is strong. Getting even may give you a short-term high, but it won't solve your problems and it may make them worse. Retaliation is a power play that invites the other person to counterattack. Someone always loses in this kind of game. Moreover, giving in to your darker self makes you unattractive. Your focus right now needs to be on taking good care of yourself, not on playing power games.

With some people, when an affair is revealed, the potential for violence is present. Usually it's the betrayed spouse who is ready to get physical, but occasionally it's the abandoned third party or even the betraying spouse. Each of you needs to identify potentially volatile situations and decide how you will act so as to prevent behavior that adds fuel to the fire or that is dangerous. Chapter Four will offer you help if this is your situation.

Forgive After You've Rebuilt Trust

"To err is human, to forgive divine."[1] But although forgiving may be divine, forgiving prematurely is unproductive. It's a way of running away from the pain, of trying to push your problems away without facing them.

If you are the one who had the affair, you will be tempted to apologize as soon as the affair is discovered, and your partner may be tempted to accept your apology and join you in sweeping the issues under the rug. Since the two of you are not able to trust each other at this point, kissing and making up is not a good idea for now. By quickly pretending the affair is behind you, you will miss out on this opportunity to resolve long-standing problems. Until you fully understand and have resolved the issues surfaced by the affair, true forgiveness is not possible.

Count on at least a year, more likely two, to resolve the basic issues in your relationship—considerably more if you are dealing with an Exit Affair where divorce issues are piled on top of the affair, or with a Sexual Addiction or a Split Self Affair where the psychological issues go deeper.

Guidelines for the Early Days

In the early days after the affair is revealed, no one knows quite what to do. When you're feeling desperate it's easy to do things you later regret. Here are some guidelines for calming the situation and staying out of trouble.

Guidelines for the Betrayed Partner

- Express your pain, anger, confusion, whatever, to your spouse, but without making threats or attacking your spouse.

- Use your support system. Get emotional support and comfort from your closest friends.

- When you find yourself ruminating about the affair (thinking, thinking, thinking . . .), look inside to see what you are feeling. Rumination is clutter, keeping you from what's important.

- Alternatively, use simple physical exercises or take walks to distract you from your rumination and to work off some anger.

- Don't use the threat of divorce out of desperation or to retaliate.

Guidelines for the Betraying Partner

- Don't get caught up in countering a threat or an attack. Don't initiate one either.
- Don't request forgiveness right now. It's too soon.
- If you want your marriage to continue, demonstrate it by being honest and forthcoming about what you are thinking, feeling, and doing.

Guidelines for Both of You

- Make no major decisions right now.
- Take no irrevocable actions right now.
- Listen to your spouse's feelings and perspective.
- Find a good therapist, someone with experience in working with couples and with affairs, and get going on resolving your issues.
- Pay attention to your emotional self. Allow yourself to grieve for your losses: your trust, your sense of belonging, your dreams, and your understanding of yourself, your partner, and your marriage. Grieving doesn't mean divorce. It means coming to terms with the emotional impact of what has happened so that you can rebuild on more solid ground.
- Don't ask anyone, especially your children, to take sides. You don't need allies; you need support and comfort.
- Talk with each other about how to explain to your children what is happening and how to reassure them. You can be sure they are picking up on your tension.
- Only if this is an Exit Affair, where the betraying partner has already decided to leave the marriage, should you get into discussions of separation and divorce right now.

- This is not the time for either of you to take a trip that keeps you from having to deal with the other.

- Both of you need to be able to talk to someone you trust. Reach an agreement on who each of you will confide in.

Affairs Happen. . . . Why?

Affairs happen. . . . With some guidelines in place, it's now time to take a quick look at why affairs happen. Affairs happen to good people. Of course, they don't just happen, even though it feels like it. Most married people never expect to have an affair. It's something you read about in the paper, something that happens to other people. When *you* have an affair, or your spouse does, you're not prepared. You don't know how to make sense of it. However, affairs are common—two out of three married couples will experience an affair at least once during their marriage. So will many other couples in committed relationships. It's how you deal with it that matters.

You've heard lots of explanations for why affairs occur. Many of them point the finger ("That tramp was out to get him"), draw moral lessons ("Adulterers will be dealt with by God"), or evade the issue ("That's just the way men are"). Recently, "It's in the genes," is back in vogue. You don't have to fall for any of these rigid ideas.

Your marital crisis actually started before the affair began. An affair means something significant is going on—or not going on—between you and your spouse. Instead of addressing the problems between you, one or both of you drifted toward an affair. In a way the affair is an attempt to solve a problem, but when you're not clear about the problem, you're not able to choose a suitable solution.

When Don told Becky, "It just happened," he truly believed that "it just happened." But affairs don't just happen. Don's affair was a long time in the making. Ever since the honeymoon ended,

Don and Becky have been ducking their conflicts and their differences. Little annoyances are withheld while both "make nice." They pride themselves on not fighting. Since they get along so well, Becky wonders why they don't feel closer. Don blames himself when he gets irritated with Becky and then he distracts himself with other activities. Recently these activities include Margie. By having an affair, Don avoids confronting Becky directly and evades for the moment his own angry feelings. Don is saying symbolically to Becky, "I'll make you pay attention to me."

Affairs only make sense when you learn about your emotional self. Even though affairs look like they happen easily, for flimsy and selfish reasons, most husbands and wives don't break their marital vows lightly. Affairs are a way of surfacing emotional problems that you haven't faced or don't know how to address. Affairs occur when you don't have the ability to verbalize your feelings, or you've been taught, "Don't say anything that's not nice," or you're afraid to risk telling your partner that you disagree. They also occur when you are driven by feelings that you don't fully understand. As a method for surfacing emotional problems, an affair is one of the most painful and difficult ways possible. However, it's one that works. An affair does get a spouse's attention.

The Road Map from Betrayal to Resolution

Affairs, even one-night stands, are more than just a blip on the calendar. Like plants, they have roots and stages of development, a life cycle, if you will, and they have an impact on others who are nearby.

The Roots of the Affair

The process that makes you vulnerable to an affair begins long before an affair is ever considered. As kids, we learn ways of dealing with people and coping with problems. Often we don't learn some of the skills we need, and we develop coping styles that don't work well in an intimate relationship. Even when you have an image of how you want your marriage to be, you don't know how to make it what you want. If you grew up in a family that suppressed differences and disagreements, you know how to be nice but not how to deal with the inevitable conflicts. If you grew up with parents who fought a lot, they probably didn't know how to teach you to be nurturing or to resolve differences. If you were abused or neglected, you're likely to carry anger about the past and have difficulty being emotionally open. If a parent's neediness meant that you had to look out for Mom or Dad, you may be a great caretaker but know little about your own needs or how to meet them. These are the patterns that you play out together in your marriage and that set up situations that can lead to an affair.

If you are a Conflict Avoider, you are likely to let troubling things go, put off talking about yourself, and coast along. You rationalize any sense of discomfort, telling yourself, "This isn't a good time, it isn't that important, I don't want to stir things up right now." When morning comes and the situation is the same, you decide that the weekend is a better time to talk. On the weekend you stay busy with the kids' activities. You may rationalize, "If she isn't worried, then neither am I," or "I don't want to hurt his feelings." Any frustration gets buried—until it gets acted out with an affair.

Or maybe you and your partner are Intimacy Avoiders and you fight all the time, with each of you afraid to give up your power. You know you have a problem, but you don't know exactly what it is or how to fix it. You dump it on your partner, your partner dumps it back, and the two of you get caught up in the fight itself rather than examining what's driving the power struggle.

If you are a Sexual Addict or the spouse of one, your inner pain and emptiness run deep because of unfinished business from childhood such as abuse, abandonment, loss, or addiction. For each of you, your behavior (the addictive behavior and the spouse's efforts to counter it), are a way to numb the pain and fill the emptiness for a brief moment.

With a Split Self Affair, you each learned early in life to devote yourself to family and suppress your own emotional needs. However, the sacrifice of self has taken a toll over the years. If you are the betraying spouse, your affair meets long-ignored emotional needs. As the betrayed spouse you may have somewhat offset the costs by turning to your children for emotional support.

As the betraying spouse in an Exit Affair, you have decided to end your marriage and you believe that you need a good reason for doing so. You present the affair to your spouse as the reason the marriage is ending, and your spouse usually accepts that as the reason. Then neither of you has to examine your own contribution to the problems in your marriage.

While it's not always obvious to the outside observer, it's important for couples facing an affair to remember that there are real problems that led to the affair. As you address your issues, unraveling these problematic roots will facilitate making the necessary changes in your life.

Stages of Development

The process of moving from betrayal to resolution goes through five stages, over the course of one to two years or more.

The Affair Begins. You probably didn't go out looking for an affair, but the option of an affair is always available. Some other wandering soul is just waiting to fill the void. You are particularly vulnerable when things are off track at home. When you feel needy you want to know that *someone* thinks you're special. When you suppress your feelings of discomfort you disable your internal "early warning system" that could tell you that you're heading for trouble.

Affairs can begin without your noticing. You may confide in a friend of the opposite sex, or let a friend pamper you, without being honest with yourself about the sexual overtones. You justify the friendship to yourself while continuing to suppress your uncomfortable feelings. You stop mentioning your friend to your spouse. The relationship begins to take on a life of its own. It feels good and it is compelling. It's been a long time since you've talked to anyone so easily. It's all so easy—first talk, then making plans to get together. Next thing you know, you're involved sexually.

Or maybe you avoid your discomfort at home by fantasizing about your ideal partner. Along comes a person who fits your fantasy and whose visions of being loved and cherished mesh with your own. You attach your dreams to this person and soon the two of you begin living a secret, secluded second life.

The Affair Is Revealed. Whether or not you, the betraying spouse, decide to reveal your affair, it is usually only a matter of time. You may, subconsciously on purpose, leave unmistakable clues, like giving your spouse a sexually transmitted disease. Or your spouse puts the pieces together and knows. A friend may tell your spouse. Your spouse may encounter you with the third party, in person or on the Internet. There are infinite ways in which affairs come to light.

Crisis in the Marriage. When the shock of disclosure wears off, chaos takes over. Intense emotional pain is accompanied by fear about what will happen to each of you and to your marriage. Rage and rumination run rampant. It feels as if everything in your life is out of control. This is the time when you're most at risk of making poor choices. The only decision you need to make right now is whether you are going to face your situation and work toward resolving the emotional problems that need attention.

Rebuilding, Together or Apart. Rebuilding means addressing and resolving your own individual issues that intertwine with your spouse's issues to become marital issues. Rebuilding requires understanding your role in what has happened and making changes in how you live your life. You will need to modify outdated behavior patterns that are getting in your way. You may succeed in rebuilding your marriage. Alternatively, you may decide to end your marriage.

You will need to become aware of the difference between thoughts and feelings, between your rational self and your emotional self. Both parts of you are essential but they work in very different ways, they give you different information, and they are good at different things. An affair is a signal that you have neglected caring for your emotional self.

For example, the work ahead for Becky and Don (who are Conflict Avoiders) is learning to pay attention to uncomfortable emotions, and developing the skills for resolving conflicts. This means taking the risk of exposing how they really feel and what they really want. Although they bragged for years about how they never fought, what they didn't say was that there was so much tension between them that they avoided talking to each other. The pressure grew but their family rules say, "Be nice—no direct conflict permitted here." Both quietly backed off to their corners in hopes that somehow they could avoid the conflict brewing in the center of the room. Of course, it's impossible for them to tackle their real issues from the corners. Without facing their conflict, there is no way out. The affair takes the covers off the conflict.

Other couples face different tasks, depending on the type of affair. Carol and Tom, who as Intimacy Avoiders are terrified of getting too close, need to risk sharing their vulnerable selves and learn how to back off without using affairs to do so. Sexual Addicts and their spouses need to heal the deep pain stemming from the chaotic and abusive childhood experiences that drive their behavior. Split Selves must give up the fantasy of the partner who will make them feel alive, and instead reclaim their own emotional selves. Exit Affairs bring the couple face to face with making practical decisions about separating and divorcing, while grieving and letting go.

Forgiveness and Closure. Forgiveness is possible, but not until you both have resolved the issues that led to the affair. Rebuilding trust takes time and attention. Then you're ready to forgive and be forgiven. Because the tendency to hold on and retaliate or to let go and forgive will be a pattern for the future, learning to forgive is important.

With forgiveness, the affair moves from being part of your present life to becoming part of your history. This changes the power balance between you—you can't use the affair any longer for leverage. If you've reached the point of forgiveness and decided to continue your marriage, it will be a different marriage than it was before: stronger, more open, and more intimate.

If the affair is an Exit Affair and your marriage has ended, forgiveness takes longer. Yet it is possible—even essential—to forgive and be forgiven. Forgiving is what frees you to move ahead unencumbered by the baggage of resentment. Resentment keeps you mired in the past, stewing over old hurts, rather than mining the gold that is to be found in difficult experiences.

Impact on Others

At the beginning of an affair you assume that no one other than you and your affair partner will ever know about the affair. This is highly unlikely. An affair is much easier to spot than those involved believe. In addition to your spouse, everyone else who is close to you is likely to experience the fallout from your affair: your children, your friends and relatives, and your work colleagues. Even those who don't know about the affair are affected by the tension, the time constraints, and the lies. Those that know the true story may feel sad, torn, anxious, or angry, even when they love you. If you've lied to them as well, coming clean with them will be part of the work ahead of you.

Summary

If an affair is in your life now, you are at a crucial turning point. The fate of your marriage is probably unknown as yet. You're afraid of what comes next. However, you are not alone with your feelings.

No one in this life escapes pain and loss. Whether you've done the betraying or been betrayed, it's important to know that you can heal from this wound. Right now, the question facing you is *will you?* Will you risk confronting what lies beneath the affair? Will you confront your own issues so that you can begin healing and learn how to feel alive again? You have a choice. I encourage you to accept the challenge of your crisis, so that you can put your pain and your anger to use in making needed changes.

Chapter Four

Flashpoints for Violence

Affairs are the catalyst for many crimes of passion.
Where did the anger start and how are you going
to handle it?

Violence related to affairs doesn't occur just in murder mysteries or the movies. The media let us know that triangles are fertile grounds for violence and murder. The danger isn't always to "some stranger, someone who's not like me." Violence occurs more often between those who know each other than between strangers, especially violence against women.[1] Violence is a possibility for anyone involved in an affair. All sides of the triangle are vulnerable. Money, prestige, and education don't lessen rage.

If your partner is having an affair, you'll certainly feel rage and you might even play out images of torture in your mind—but you're unlikely to carry out your fantasies. Few betrayed spouses actually come close—but some do.

Because many people don't report affair-related violence, either believing it is a personal matter or fearing retaliation, it is impossible to know the true extent of such violence. However for every person murdered over an affair, several more experience serious violence. Still others are the target of attacks that are thwarted, interrupted, or otherwise derailed.

The catalyst in affair-related violence is rage at being betrayed, the essence of which is feeling abandoned and humiliated. Research indicates that abandonment and powerlessness are linked to extreme violence,[2] and that family members and other intimates are the most common victims of murder.[3] For the person who is emotionally fragile, betrayal has as much to do with perception as with reality. The fact that the spouses have separated doesn't lessen the pain and rage of being betrayed. In fact, separation is likely to exaggerate such feelings. Just because a person has never been violent doesn't mean that violence can't occur this time.

Why do some people act out their rage while others don't? The difference is linked primarily to the depth of unresolved ego wounds from the past, whether a support system exists, the use of alcohol or drugs, the presence of weapons, and how this wound—the abandonment and humiliation stemming from the affair—is handled.

Our society's attitudes about affairs sometimes encourage violence. We judge, ridicule, punish, and blame those who have affairs and their spouses. Talk of violence is rampant, not just in response to affairs, but generally. We glorify violence, often rationalizing it as a just response to acts of betrayal or even disrespect. Spousal abuse is only beginning to be taken seriously.

Many states' divorce laws still incorporate extra punishment for adultery. In the wake of recent "sex scandals," a number of military officers were court-martialed or discharged after being charged with adultery and related offenses. The Defense Department has since banned close or intimate contact between officers and subordinates in the military, with punishment options ranging from prison to a dishonorable discharge.[4]

Factors That Contribute to Violence

Betrayal is no joke for the person on the receiving end. An affair, when combined with certain situational and personality factors, increases the likelihood of violence. Violence is most likely to occur among Exiters, Intimacy Avoiders, and Conflict Avoiders. With an Exit Affair, the loss of the marriage compounds the betrayal, and the legal process of divorce may further escalate the situation. Intimacy Avoiders are battlers to begin with, and their battles escalate easily. Conflict Avoiders do not intend to become violent, but those who bottle up their emotions too severely and for too long may explode.

Some people who become physically violent have a history of spouse abuse or other violent behavior. Others have never been physical.[5] When they do explode it's because they have reached their breaking point. An affair is the kind of crisis that can push a person over the edge.

While we can't know for sure whether violence will erupt within a particular triangle, we can assess the potential for violence and take precautions to prevent or minimize violence. Assessing the potential means looking at situational and personality factors.

No matter which role in the triangle is yours, you may be at risk. If you're the betraying spouse, your partner may be sufficiently enraged to become violent with you. You might also be targeted as the villain by your affair partner's spouse. And, if you end the affair, your affair partner may feel so abandoned and humiliated that he or she resorts to violence directed at you.

If you are the betrayed spouse, violence could come from the third party who is furious at you for not getting out of the picture. If you are the third party, your primary risk of violence comes from the betrayed spouse who is enraged and blames you for what has happened.

Any time that rage is combined with a loss of control, the elements of destruction are present. Add alcohol or drugs plus a weapon and there's bound to be an explosion unless active measures are taken to prevent it.

Situational Factors

Situational factors that contribute to affair-specific violence are events associated with abandonment, humiliation, or helplessness, the presence or absence of social supports, and the availability of weapons. The most common precipitants are discovery of the spouse's affair, marital separation, or a loss in court. Even in divorces without an affair and with no history of violence, a higher-than-average potential for violence is present.[6]

The Exit Affair incorporates both an affair and divorce. For the abandoned spouse, the double betrayal of being dumped for another person makes for a deep rage. Feelings of abandonment, helplessness, and humiliation abound and it's easy to believe that there's nothing left to lose. The final straw can be anything that escalates these feelings, that takes away the normal sense of control—something as simple as finding the checking account is overdrawn or as heavy as finding your spouse with the affair partner. Other losses at this time, such as the loss of a job or the death of a family member, can also strike the match. These are the true "crimes of passion" rather than random or premeditated violence.

In many cases, our legal system further escalates the odds of violence. The emphasis on right and wrong and the use of procedures that are invasive and demeaning combine to give hurt partners the idea that they can be vindicated. The opportunity for custody and money contests, requiring one partner to prove the other is malicious or corrupt or both, brings out the worst in everyone and is traumatizing for children. Even though many courts have gotten away from the worst features of the adversarial divorce, some divorce attorneys still encourage their clients to ravage the other spouse, no matter what the emotional or financial cost.

Some betrayed spouses choose this method of retaliating. They engage in custody battles focused on gaining sole custody or on preventing contact between the children and the spouse's new partner, or they may attempt to strip the betraying spouse financially. Betraying spouses can also engage in this kind of retaliation. People who get caught up in retaliating are those who have not faced their losses. Instead they've gotten stuck in "attack mode" and are using it to deflect their pain. The help they need is with their grief, not another highly charged legal maneuver. If you're considering using the legal system to get even, be careful. Doing so can precipitate violence in someone who is emotionally fragile.

Personality Factors

Personality factors play a significant role in violence. People who become violent do so because they haven't learned safe ways to deal with the powerful emotions that are set off by a crisis. The intense pain of being abandoned, the impotent rage of feeling humiliated, the jealous anger at being betrayed, or the frightened fury at finding oneself powerless demand an outlet. For some people, the only response they know is to take physical action in an attempt to stop the inner devastation and gain some control over the situation. Those most likely to become violent have many of the following characteristics and patterns of behavior:

- Act out emotions rather than talk about them
- Are rigid or controlling
- Are obsessive
- Lack friends and are somewhat isolated
- Have low self esteem
- Display bullying behavior
- Are easily upset
- Currently feel betrayed, abandoned, or humiliated
- Have difficulty managing feelings of helplessness or powerlessness
- Had difficulty coping emotionally with past crises
- Feel there is nothing left to lose

- Have a history of physical violence, explosive temper, or rages
- Have a history of acquiescing and bottling up feelings
- Have a history of severe manic or paranoid behavior
- Have made threats
- Use alcohol or drugs
- Own a gun
- Witnessed or experienced physical violence in family of origin

Overall, the personality is rather rigid and controlling combined with a brittle quality, as if the person could easily explode. You may feel reluctant to push anything with this person because you sense that they could easily lose control. Honor that sense of wariness. Keep in mind, however, that having these characteristics does not mean a person *will* become violent; rather it is a statement about a possibility—a possibility that you do not want to test.

Managing the Situation to Prevent Violence

Whichever part of the triangle is yours, what do you need to do to prevent violence? Preventing violence means taking steps to defuse the situation, whether you are the betrayer, the betrayed, or the third party. There are many things you can do but you may also need to get outside help.

A Basic Rule for Preventing Violence

Don't strip the other person. Feeling they have nothing left to lose increases the risk of that person becoming violent. This means don't take away their fragile self-esteem by humiliating or shaming them, avoid removing things they value, don't threaten them, and don't punish them financially in or out of court. It means no attacks, no surprises. You probably know what will set your partner off. Make sure you don't do it.

Ways the Betraying Spouse Can Prevent Violence

If you are the betraying partner, what can you do to keep from provoking a violent reaction from your partner?

- Be honest. Take responsibility for what you've done. It's the lying and the avoidance that most disturb your partner.
- Don't blame your partner for causing you to have an affair. While both of you set the stage by not dealing with the issues between you, you are the one that chose to deal with the situation by having the affair.
- Don't rub your affair in your partner's face. Humiliation will further enrage your spouse.
- Acknowledge how hurt and angry your partner is. Make statements like, "I can see that I've really hurt you." This way you connect at the emotional level, and your partner may recognize that you do recognize his or her pain.
- Don't try to "fix it," or explain or justify your affair to your spouse. That will be infuriating to a spouse who wants you to hear what he or she is feeling.
- Don't compare your partner with the third party, positively or negatively.
- Don't add insult to injury, either verbally or by your actions.
- Don't trap your spouse. Leave options and escape routes open. When people perceive they have options they are less likely to resort to violence.
- Be respectful—your partner is a person.
- Get any weapons out of the house or lock them up. Many homicides would not have occurred if a weapon had not been handy.

Ways the Third Party Can Prevent Violence

If you're the third party, you too may be a potential target for violence. To keep yourself as safe as possible, observe the following guidelines.

- Do not call your affair partner's residence.
- Do not call or otherwise contact the spouse of your affair partner.
- If the spouse of your affair partner contacts you, be respectful, take responsibility for your role, and end the discussion.
- Do not tell others about personal matters of your affair partner's spouse.
- Don't criticize your affair partner's spouse to anyone.
- Consider taking a break from the affair.

Ways the Betrayed Spouse Can Prevent Violence

When you've been betrayed, it's common to think about doing damage to your spouse or to the third party. Most people manage to avoid acting on such thoughts, but with the wrong combination of emotions and circumstances, you could lose control. You need to take steps to ensure that your violent feelings remain feelings and that you don't act upon them. The next section provides guidance for dealing safely with your rage.

You also risk being the target of violence. Many of the guidelines already given for the betraying spouse and the third party will be useful for you too in defusing potential violence directed toward you.

When You're the One at Risk of Losing Control

Whichever part of the triangle is yours, you may be the person at risk of losing control. If you're on the edge, one inclination is to take control, to do something, almost anything so as not to feel helpless. A cooling-off period can allow your wiser self to prevail.

Another tendency is to pursue "justice." Mix in rage, and this can be a deadly combination. This kind of search for justice is propelled by extreme rage combined with righteousness. You lose all perspective, especially if "seeking justice" becomes your cause. Your target may be your spouse, the third party, or yourself.

- If you are on the verge of losing control, *get help immediately.* Call a hotline or 911, call a trusted friend, go to the emergency room or the local mental health center. Call a cab if you're beyond driving. You are responsible for taking whatever action is required to maintain control, no matter how enraged you are.
- Stay out of situations that you know will inflame you. That probably means keeping your distance from the other members of the triangle.
- When you find yourself ruminating about being violent, change gears. Call a friend, go for a walk, or do something different that disrupts your train of thought.
- If you know you have a problem with anger, don't wait until you are enraged to get help. Get yourself to a therapist who can help you deal safely with your rage.
- Learn and use simple anger exercises, such as hitting a punching bag.
- Make it your policy to take a time-out when you're angry.
- Avoid alcohol, drugs, and driving when you're angry.
- Ask a trusted friend or relative to take any weapons out of your house and put them in safekeeping.
- Remind yourself that hurting others or yourself won't solve anything—learning how to take care of yourself is what will help.

When You Face a Potentially Violent Situation

How do you know if you're at risk? Indicators include threats made by the other spouse or the third party, stalking or other bizarre behavior by that person, or a gut sense that their rage is about to go out of control. *Always trust that gut sense.* Sometimes you may not be aware that you are at risk. If you identify with *any* of the risk factors mentioned in this chapter, it's best to act at all times as if you're at risk.

What do you do when you are at risk? You stay out of range, you avoid any provocative behavior, and you get immediate professional help. Take action to ensure your own safety before you are in a critical situation. Once you're in danger, your options are greatly limited. Talk to a counselor who specializes in domestic violence, and follow up on recommendations such as getting a restraining order or going to a shelter (shelters are usually an option only for women). Hotlines are another valuable resource that can offer you guidance for staying safe.

If a potentially violent situation occurs anyway, keep the following advice in mind:

- If you can, leave, and then call 911 or a hotline.
- If you can't leave, call 911 or a hotline.
- Do not ever try to take a weapon from an enraged person.
- Don't argue with someone who is in a rage. Repeat what was said and no more. For example, suppose your partner is screaming, "You are nothing but a no-good piece of trash." Repeat in a neutral tone of voice, "You think I'm nothing but a no-good piece of trash." This lets the person know you've heard them but it doesn't challenge them. Challenging someone who is in a rage will escalate the rage and can precipitate physical violence. You will be perceived as challenging if you attempt to correct misinformation, claim that everything will be OK, say you're sorry, or make promises for the future. Obviously, if you get angry that will escalate the danger. The only safe response is to repeat what they've said. Use a soothing tone of voice and give the person a way to save face.
- Don't ask the enraged person to justify their anger or prove anything. Agree with them: "Yes, you're right." "Yes, I

understand." Absolutely don't say, "Yes, but—" This is not the time to argue.

- Don't try to persuade the raging person to give up his or her anger. When someone is raging they are usually unaware that their judgment is off. Let whoever responds to your 911 call (probably the police) or hotline intervene. They are experienced in identifying the phase of aggression and intervening accordingly. Among their strategies are defusing the rage by repeating or "yessing" or gently helping the enraged person consider those that care about him, his children for example, and the effect on them of any violence.

- Keep the person talking in order to buy time. Being enraged takes tremendous energy, and there are physical limits as to how long that level of energy expenditure can be maintained. Once the person begins to come down from the peak of their rage, stop talking and let them calm down. Real talking comes after that. *Get immediate help* from a professional for this discussion.

Summary

The emotions of betrayal are intense. When the wrong combination of provocations and personalities comes together, the situation can escalate and ignite. Each person involved in an affair is responsible for keeping the situation safe. Consider what you may need to do to make your situation safe, and take the required steps promptly.

Chapter Five

Letting Go of Obsession

Continuing to nurse your wound has its own life,
which deprives you of a real life. Having your own
life gives you a destination.

If only you could go backward to a time when things made sense!
Or get things under control now. Your mind circles endlessly, looking for explanations. Meanwhile you straighten up the family
room, put that dish in its place, tell yourself not to forget to pick up
the kids at day care, get things in order, stave off disaster. On the
near side of order is chaos. Feelings of loss and abandonment lurk
around the edges. What does all this mean? Your dreams have gone
up the chimney—will your marriage follow? Or will you be able to
hold it together? You obsess and obsess and obsess some more about
your partner's affair.

Learning about your partner's affair is devastating. After the
shock and disbelief of discovery come pain and anger. Your distress
is so excruciatingly intense that you set it aside in hopes that getting the facts and knowing why this happened will ease your pain.
But nothing makes sense. Trust goes out the door and obsessing
about the affair prevails. Obsessing keeps your spouse on the defensive, at a distance, groveling and guilty—you hope.

Nan screamed at Phil as she flung the Visa bill at him: "How
could you! You've been lying to me all this time. You're not the person I thought you were. You're just a cheat. You're just like all the
other men who cheat on their wives. And to think that I trusted
you!" She goes on, "Just what did you have on your mind? Wasn't

I good enough? What makes her so special? Is she better in bed? How could you do this to me?"

Nan's obsessive rage is typical of someone who has recently learned of a spouse's affair. It is as if by learning about every detail, every kiss, every word, the affair can be put in its place. It can't. This approach will drive you as crazy as it will your spouse. And don't say, "Good, it's worth it!" There is no need to sacrifice your sanity just for revenge.

In this chapter we will first focus on the purpose of obsession, and then explore how to shift from your head to your heart. Finally we will examine the emotional path the two of you traveled to reach this painful and life-changing place.

The Nature of Obsession

For the betrayed spouse, obsessing keeps the deeper pain at bay—maybe if you can understand the affair rationally there's a safe way out. Obsessing feels awful but it offers the illusion of answers, answers that seem almost within reach. But obsessing doesn't work. Feeling your pain is the only path that will allow you to begin healing.

The Feel of Obsession

Obsession is a way of keeping it all in your head—it's safer there. Being rational feels safe so you ruminate endlessly, going over every detail of the past. Staying in your head pushes away your pain and fear and keeps your anger at a far distance. But when you let the pain creep in—what then? Pain means facing the fact that things are not as you have believed, and not as you want. Pain means things are badly off track. When you are alone with your pain, when your partner won't share in your pain or even acknowledge that you're hurting and have a reason to hurt, it is a very lonely time indeed. Loneliness builds, anger creeps in. And this is the danger point. Will you go out of control? What will contain your pain?

Can your pain be shoved back inside? Or is your pain out in the open for good? What now? How to contain it? You turn to your spouse with your accusations and tirades, looking for acknowledgment. None to be had. Your partner says, "You're just jealous; you're insecure"—and your anger escalates. You proclaim, "You're telling me I'm jealous and insecure! You're the one who had the affair. Don't you try and make me feel guilty for what you've done!" This twist of the knife fuels your fire. Your anger is coming. Watch out! Here it comes! Get out of the way, everyone! You're going to tell the world just how awful your spouse has been.

This is obsessive rage rather than an expression of what you're feeling. It's clear that you're angry, but with obsessive rage you are saying more about what your spouse has done than about you and how you feel.

Shifting from Obsession to Emotion

Going numb and then going nuts is the typical pattern when you learn about your spouse's affair. Everything feels chaotic. One minute you're in a rage, the next you're bawling like a baby, and a moment later you're talking revenge. You're obsessed with knowing every detail of the affair. Maybe, if you just knew more about it, you could get a handle on this nightmare. Maybe, if you just understood, life could go back to the way it was. If only you could get the facts right! You ask and ask—nothing makes sense. You know that your spouse is getting fed up with your inquisition but you can't stop.

Actually the facts won't do you much good. You need to face your emotions to begin healing. Pain and anger are your best allies—they are real and they are powerful. They create a fortress designed to energize you and to protect you against further hurt. You also need to reach an emotional understanding of how the two of you got here, and this takes time. Fear pushes at you: fear that your marriage is done for, apprehension that life as you know it is over. Now that this has happened, what's the point? Maybe you should just cut your losses and end the marriage before your partner does that too.

Don't let your fear take over. Now is the time to slow down. Even though you're feeling devastated and are desperate to get things settled, you need to take it slow and easy.

- Take off the close-up lens and put on a wide-angle one. You can't see the whole marriage if you're looking only at one part.

- This is not the time for major decisions. Decisions driven by an emotional crisis tend to be poor ones because you lack information and objectivity.

- Find out what the affair in your life means. You may find that neither of you wants the marriage to end, although you don't know quite how to move ahead. Or it may be that your partner's affair really is the announcement that your marriage is ending.

- Take your time and allow yourself to feel your way carefully.

Whether or not your marriage continues, you are facing major changes in your life. Right now you don't know where reality is. You can no longer rely on your long-standing beliefs and assumptions about your partner or your marriage. Your dreams for the future are also jeopardized. With all this at stake, you will want to take enough time to sort through what has happened so that you can make good choices for yourself. As you do, new options will open.

If your marriage has a chance of making it, your next moves are critical. It is easy to sabotage yourself. Think smart. Keep in mind that a "hired gun" type of attorney won't save you from your pain. Obsessing about your spouse's guilt and your innocence are equally useless because they keep you from understanding why this has happened. Focusing on the third party won't help either. Instead, pay attention to your pain, your fear, and your anger, keeping in mind that anger is not the same thing as blame, retaliation, or revenge.

Let your real feelings be your guide. What is your physical self telling you about what you feel? Are you tied up in knots, or do you feel like crying? Are you hurt? Scared? Angry? Obsessing seems to be about your feelings but it is not. Obsession is part of your thinking process and it actually keeps you away from your emotions and distracts you from your own agenda. Obsessing is like putting a canvas bag over your feelings at the very time they need the bright light of day. Obsessing about the affair will be your biggest obstacle.

Equally dangerous to your emotional health is letting your panic push you into accepting a premature apology. Post warning flags if you're tempted to forgive and forget before you understand how you got here.

The Patterns and Purposes of Obsession

What is obsession? Obsession is thinking about something over and over again, trying to make rational sense of it. Obsession means ruminating, speculating, blaming, hanging on like a dog with a bone. You get revved up when you obsess, but you're not in touch with your feelings. When you're pursuing details, denouncing your spouse, and attempting to substantiate your case, you're like a squirrel chasing its tail in circles on an exercise wheel—and you end up just as exhausted as the squirrel.

At first the obsessive questioning is a reality check. In looking backward, one man described his reaction to learning of his wife's affair: "I thought I had a great marriage. We were super communicators; we cared about each other; we both had good jobs; our life was in order. And then I found out that my reality wasn't reality at all. I had to find out where reality was. How far off base was I? That's what all the questions were about."

Initially, obsession serves as a protection of sorts. It's a way of delaying the reality of where you are. It says, "This is not the way things are supposed to be. Somebody—make it right!" Obsession is also a way of saying that you are innocent, that this breakdown in your marriage is not your doing, it is totally your spouse's fault—and it wouldn't have happened if that despicable less-than-a-person third party hadn't lured your partner into a trap.

Your obsessing begins to take on a life of its own. You ask your spouse question after question about the affair. You ask the same questions again because whatever your partner says is not enough. "Did she make the first move? What did you say to her? What's wrong with me that you could do this to me? Where did you go together? How could you take her there? What was so special about her? Why didn't you tell me if you thought things weren't right? When did you see her last? Are you still seeing her? How can I believe that? How many times did you have sex? What does she have that I don't have? How could you do this to me? Do you love her?"

Your wake your spouse up at 3 A.M., insisting, "We have to talk now!" You ask, "Was she better in bed than I am?" No matter what your partner says, you lose: If he says yes you're devastated and if he says no, you don't believe him. You accuse him of never being honest, of thinking about the other woman, of not caring about your feelings, and of betraying you at every turn. You think about the affair so much that it becomes your life. You're so obsessed that it's as if you're having an affair with the affair.

It's tempting to stay with this type of questioning. It provides the illusion of understanding and it makes your partner squirm. Obsessing at this point is similar to what your partner was doing in having the affair: it is a way of avoiding the difficult issues, and it blocks your potential for resolving the real issues. Obsessive discussion of the affair pushes everything else out of the picture. Getting answers to questions like "How many times did you have sex with him?" won't help you understand. Now that you know how many times, what do you know? Right now you probably aren't going to believe anything your partner says, anyway. Asking such questions gives your partner the chance to blow off the real issues. Allison confessed, "Sure, I answered his questions about where we went. Those are the easy questions. I was relieved when he let me slide."

Even if avoiding heavy emotional stuff worked for you while you were growing up, it will keep you stuck now. If your spouse doesn't have to listen to how you feel and you don't have to take any responsibility for repairing the marriage, this is a prescription for disaster. If you want the marriage, both of you will need to look at how together you created a big enough hole in your marriage for a third party. Yes, the person who had the affair is responsible for making that choice, but affairs don't happen in marriages without space for them. The space between you and your spouse had probably become dead space, a gap between you that neither one acknowledged or knew how to bridge.

How is obsessing different from expressing your feelings? Obsessing occurs when you use your rational mind to tackle an emotional problem. Obsessing is a way of trying to distance your pain and stay in control; it keeps you from having to stay with your own feelings. The hope is that if you could just understand what happened, then maybe you can put the affair in its place and make everything better again. You keep mulling over the facts, trying to make them come out differently, but this approach just leaves you more exhausted and confused. Affairs are about feelings, and rational thinking doesn't resolve emotional issues. Continuing to *think* about the affair will keep you in the squirrel cage. Letting your emotional process go to work is the only thing that will help.

It's only when you sit with your feelings that you discover what you're really afraid of—and it's not the affair or the third party. It goes much deeper, to your own weaknesses, uncertainties, and insecurities. If you are continuing to obsess about your partner's affair months after you learned about it, consider the possibility that you are hanging on to it as a way of staving off your pain and fear about deeper issues. Are you willing to give up painting the Scarlet A across your spouse's chest? If not, this marriage won't work. By obsessing, you override all else.

When You Are Obsessing About Your Partner's Affair

Getting out of the obsessive cycle requires that you make a decision to do so. It won't just happen. However, once you decide to change directions, you can open yourself to new ways of giving your self a voice.

Self-Assessment

Let's look at your motivations for continuing along the same obsessive path, and why you might choose to change directions. Mentally check off all the following factors that are true for you, and add any others:

Reasons you want to continue obsessing:

- You want to punish your spouse.
- Obsessing helps you avoid feeling out of control or helpless.
- Obsessing helps you avoid your own pain or fear.
- You believe that understanding what happened will lead to a solution.
- You're not ready to face the deeper marital problems.
- You're afraid of losing your partner's attention.
- You think your partner should take care of you.
- You want to make your partner stay in the marriage.
- And . . .
- And also . . .

Reasons you want to stop obsessing:

- Your spouse may get sick enough of your obsession to leave you.
- Obsessing leaves you exhausted.
- You dislike yourself when you obsess.
- Your friends are getting fed up with listening to you.

- It's hurting your kids.
- You don't want to sabotage whatever potential your marriage holds.
- You want to feel better.
- And . . .
- And also . . .

If you're having trouble finding any reasons to stop obsessing and the affair is not new news, consider seeing a therapist to help you get unstuck.

What Do You Need to Do?

So you're sick of obsessing! Let's talk about what else you can do. First of all, you could put your inquisition about the affair aside and shift your focus from preventing future betrayals to shoring up your marriage. If you have real questions about the affair (as opposed to obsessive questions), you can come back to them later. Next, since you can only change yourself, you can focus on the changes that will help you be the person you want to be. If your partner is also willing to work, the two of you can work together, but you are only responsible for changing yourself. Neither of you can fix the other, or "fix it" for them. Your immediate agenda is to learn how to pay attention to your emotions, and how to give yourself a voice.

How do you give yourself a voice? To have a voice, you have to know how you feel. If your spouse has had an affair, it's going to be very important that you pay attention to those feelings that you have ignored: anxiety and fear, disappointment, hurt and pain, sadness, and anger. From there you can begin to voice your feelings as well as your thoughts.

It's hard work for anyone to change their way of connecting to their partner and to others, particularly about difficult issues. An affair is probably the most difficult of all issues. However, when you meet this challenge, it's emotionally satisfying and self-validating.

Most important, changing the way you relate is absolutely necessary for moving ahead, individually or together.

Pay Attention to Your Emotions. The invisible virus that got into your marriage and had you both avoiding the tough emotional issues before the affair is not going to suddenly disappear. You've got work to do on giving your emotions their due. Are you able to recognize and put a name to what you are feeling? Or has your pattern been to ignore your emotions? Do you sometimes wonder why you don't feel more? Do you put your feelings aside so as not to hurt others or because you fear their response?

We were all born with the capacity to feel and to express our feelings. Just look at how a baby lets its parents know when it is hungry or uncomfortable. People *learn* how to suppress their feelings. Perhaps you grew up in a family where no one talked about emotions, and you learned the family pattern. Or your experience may have been one of being overburdened with responsibility, or maybe neglected, criticized, rejected, or humiliated, or even abused. Many of us learn to suppress our painful feelings. Once this becomes a habit, suppression doesn't discriminate between positive and negative emotions. However, it's possible to change your habits and reclaim your feelings.

Right now, your pain and anger are probably the feelings you are most in touch with. When you've been betrayed, pain and anger are normal. However the difference between pain or anger and obsession is not always clear. Trust your emotional self to feel the difference. Anger is an emotion *in you*; it's not just raising your voice or trashing your partner. Anger is not something that someone has done to you. Your anger is your reaction to being hurt. When your spouse has an affair, you are deeply hurt, and your anger follows as a defense against the hurt. Paying attention to your pain and your anger is much more important than distracting yourself with another question about the third party. Your future emotional health depends on giving your pain and anger a voice.

Anger is a difficult and confusing feeling for many people. If you have trouble letting yourself feel your anger, you might start by noticing the feeling in the pit of your stomach, or the tension in your body. You can say out loud: "I am angry!" Say it as if you mean it! Yell it in the shower! Feelings of fear and powerlessness may also lie underneath your anger. Let yourself get beneath the anger so that you can feel *your* pain, *your* fear, and *your* powerlessness. It will help if you take these feelings seriously, and not trivialize them by talking about the third party or becoming the keeper of your spouse.

But you insist, "I *am* angry! Didn't you hear what I just said? I told Bob that he's lower than low. How could he do this to me?" This is a statement of your *thoughts* about Bob, not an expression of your anger. Anger sounds more like this: "I am furious at you!" or "I am angry at you for lying to me!" Pain might sound like this: "I am so hurt that you've done this." Powerlessness might be: "I don't know what to do. Nothing I do makes any difference right now." See whether your words and your tone of voice are connected to what you are feeling inside. You don't need to scream or carry on or attack your spouse to convey just how hurt and angry you are. You don't have to explain or justify your anger either. In fact, the simpler your statement, the less able your partner will be to dismiss or argue with what you are saying.

Give Yourself a Voice. Voicing your emotions means talking about how *you* feel, not about everything your spouse has done. Voicing comes with acknowledging (maybe for the first time) what you feel. Just learning to identify your feelings gives them form, and this is a critical change for you. Let your tone of voice match your words. It can be OK to yell but it's often more powerful and more effective to let the pain beneath your anger show in your inflection, your voice, the tears that come with your words, or in other ways that convey your experience. Anger is different from blame, revenge, or retaliation—it's cleaner, and less likely to elicit a counterattack. Brad confided, "Angie's affair gave me my freedom. It made it OK to be angry. It's OK to be angry about an affair."

Don't confuse real gut anger with blame or revenge. That means *no beating up on yourself or anyone else, verbally or physically.* Blaming and attacking are not expressions of anger but of obsession and they end up harming you. Especially don't settle for blaming the third party. Your spouse is the one who has betrayed you and it is your spouse who needs to listen to your pain and anger. Remember that others can't read your mind. Your spouse can't listen to your feelings if you don't voice them.

Carla, who is married to Ben, is giving voice to her feelings. Carla half cries and half yells at Ben: "I can't believe you did this to me! How could you?! I am so hurt—I am furious! To think that I trusted you—and this is what you do to me! I don't want to be near you right now. How could you do this to me? I just don't understand." Ben mumbles something about "I didn't mean to hurt you, it just happened." Carla retorts: "What do you mean it just happened! It didn't just happen—you decided to do it! I am so furious! I don't even want to talk to you now!" She is not about to let Ben get close to her when she feels so vulnerable.

Charlie, whose wife Jeanne had an affair, is not expressing his pain or his anger to her. Instead, he is reacting and attacking. Charlie's anger about Jeanne's affair is caustic and white-hot. Charlie sticks his index finger an inch from Jeanne's face and boils over with a roar: "You're nothing but a no-good tramp! You're not fit to be a parent! My sons shouldn't have to be exposed to you! You're going to pay for this!" Jeanne thrusts her shoulders forward and bites back: "Why do you think I had an affair? Having to put up with you and your criticism and your screaming day after day! Nothing I ever do pleases you. Arden knows how to treat a woman!"

Both Carla and Charlie are hurt and angry, but their ways of expressing themselves are very different. How are Carla's and Charlie's comments different? Most of Carla's comments are about her emotions. Because Carla didn't attack him, Ben doesn't need to counterattack. Thus he's left to face the pain his affair has created. Charlie, on the other hand, says nothing about his own feelings and instead goes for the jugular verbally. Charlie and Jeanne are just beginning a fight in which both of them are going to bloody each other and be bloodied. The pain in their relationship increases but is covered over by the fighting and the blaming about the affair.

Voicing your pain and anger effectively means doing it in a way that is safe and doesn't backfire. Safety has to do with what you say and how you express it. This includes your timing and location, your tone of voice, and who you talk to. These are some basic principles:

- Use "I" messages to express your pain and anger. ("I feel that you—" is not an "I" message or a feeling. "I feel angry" is a feeling and an "I" message.)
- Direct your anger at your partner, not the third party. ("I am angry at you!")
- Omit the justifications and explanations for your feelings—a simple statement that you are angry is more powerful. The justifications let your spouse avoid your main message and invite arguments about side issues.
- Choose a safe location, maybe your therapist's office, if you're afraid the situation might get out of control.
- Leave your children out of it. This means don't have this conversation when they can see or hear you—and if they're around they'll be listening.
- Pick times when neither of you is exhausted or ready to go over the edge.

It's not just big feelings like anger that need to be voiced but those small uncomfortable feelings that, if unattended, will nag until eventually they take on a life of their own. Positive feelings are generally easier to express, but sometimes we defer those too. Intimacy Avoiders in particular have difficulty sharing loving emotions or those that expose needs, desires, and vulnerabilities. You can start small in voicing your more sensitive and vulnerable side and build from there. For all of us, it's a matter of giving voice to our whole self: our feelings and our thoughts, the big issues and small discomforts we experience, and the entire range of our emotional selves from anger and pain to passion and excitement.

When Your Partner Is Obsessing About Your Affair

It can be pretty tough when your spouse is obsessing about your affair. You want the obsessing to stop. You've tried everything you know and it hasn't worked. Sandy and Dick had been married for twelve years when Sandy had an affair. Dick's obsession was going full steam within a week after learning about her affair. At first, Sandy figured she needed to pay her dues. She told herself she didn't want to hurt Dick any more than he was already hurting. Down deep she wanted to protect herself from facing Dick's real feelings of pain and anger.

Dick filled almost any lull in activity with his obsessing: "I just don't see how you could do this to me! I can't stop thinking about it. Did he tell you he loved you?" Sandy said he had. Dick went on, "Did you tell him you loved him?" Sandy squirmed, obviously uncomfortable and not wanting to answer. Dick responded, "I knew it! I don't see how we can ever put this back together! How could you do this! You've ruined everything! What's the point of even trying! I trusted you, and you go and do this. Don't you have any decency?" Sandy broke in, "Dick, I'm sorry. I know I've really hurt you and I can't change that now, but I really want to be with you and I want to work on our relationship." Dick replied, "Why didn't you think of that earlier!" This is not the first time Dick and Sandy have been through this—it's more like the hundred and fiftieth time.

Perhaps, like Sandy, you have listened to your partner obsess about your affair, you try to answer the questions, you apologize, you try to make up for it, and you try to "fix it." Still, the questions continue. You start getting impatient, "We've been over this a dozen times before. I told you the truth! There's nothing else to tell." Your partner responds, "But how can I trust you! I thought you were telling me the truth before, but you were lying to me!" You begin to feel battered by the never-ending questioning. You get defensive, avoiding your spouse when you can, appeasing when possible, and blaming when that fails. Listening to your partner's pain and anger is essential, but trying to satisfy your spouse's obsessive questions is doomed to failure.

Sandy was right on the mark when she observed to Dick, "I have to keep writing the checks. It's not just for what I did to you but for what the world did." Dick admitted that his anger kept him from feeling helpless, and that he was scared to death of being helpless because everything around him would fall apart, like it had when he was a child. Neither Sandy nor Dick has any sense of what the affair is really about. Right now, Dick's obsessing and Sandy's fear of talking honestly are getting in the way of facing reality. If this sounds like your situation, you may wonder how to deal with your partner's obsession.

Be available to listen to your spouse's pain, but once the initial shock is over, back off from your spouse's obsession. You may not always be clear about what is pain and what is obsession. Trust your gut to feel the difference. With pain, you're more likely to feel overwhelmed, afraid, guilty, sad, or ashamed of the behavior that led to your spouse's pain. Obsession is more likely to irritate or annoy you. The message that comes through to you is, in effect, "No matter what you do, it's not going to be enough." On that, your spouse is right—there is nothing you can do to adequately counter your spouse's obsession. You might consider not responding to the obsession so as not to encourage it.

Your spouse's pain is a different matter. You need to hear the pain—not fix it but hear it and take it in emotionally. When you do, you too will be in pain. It may be possible at this point to offer some comfort to each other, perhaps holding each other or crying together. Staying put and connecting with your spouse's pain is one of the most difficult things you can do right now—and one of the most important.

Starting to Put the Affair in Its Place

During the obsessive phase following the disclosure of the affair, the betraying spouse is usually not aware of the deepest reasons for the affair. The obsessive questioning doesn't help the two of you get close. Perhaps you, the betraying spouse, settle for telling yourself that you're in love or that everyone does it, that your spouse is always angry or that you're going to leave your marriage anyway. When you're the betrayed spouse, and your spouse's answers to your questions don't satisfy you, you become more agitated and obsessive, repeatedly lamenting, "How could you do this to me?" You conclude that your spouse is sick or that there is something the matter with you. You fear that the marriage is over and decide that you will never trust again. None of these interpretations does your situation justice.

It will be important to begin putting the affair in its place. That doesn't mean discussing the affair. Instead, it's taking a look at all those small and not-so-small steps that led to the affair. What were those painful occurrences that neither of you talked about? Do you know what was on your partner's mind for the year or so before the affair began? Was he hurt by your criticism? Was she afraid that you might leave her? Was she so caught up with being a mother that you were out in the cold? Was he so into career building that the only times you saw him he was exhausted or asleep? Did you find it difficult when she gave you advice? Were you resentful when he made decisions you didn't like? Did you feel powerless at times? Did you find someone who would pay attention to you after her attentions shifted to the new baby, or his career became the center of his life? What were the two of you actually talking about during this period? The difference between what was really going on for each of you before the affair and what was being talked about will tell you where some of your problems are.

Can You Talk About Old Issues in New Ways?

It will be important to find new ways to talk about these issues. See if you can take the high road, being as honest as you know how, but doing so gently.

- Can you offer reassurance along with information, rather than being brutal in your honesty?
- Can you provide information that aids in understanding what has happened, or will you be evasive?
- Can you begin talking about why an affair was your choice for avoiding the issues?
- Can you tolerate hearing your partner's pain and can you acknowledge that pain?
- Can you each share your own emotions?
- Can you each identify the changes in your relationship as you married, had children, moved, changed jobs, and grew up or didn't grow up?
- Can you begin talking about the hurts and disappointments that never got acknowledged?
- Can the two of you start talking about how things got so badly off track?

Remember Carla, whose situation was described earlier in this chapter? Carla discovered that she had ignored or dismissed her feelings for years, not wanting to feel her pain. This dated back to her childhood, when her mother had been super-critical, especially when Carla wanted attention from her father. She never realized that ignoring her feelings left her vulnerable. That is because feelings provide information that the rational mind doesn't have. Uncomfortable feelings are an early warning system, letting us know there is a problem or danger at hand. When we don't pay attention to these feelings we can find ourselves in deep water. Carla's tuning out made it impossible for her to pick up on the many clues that her husband, Ben, was dropping before and during his affair. Without knowing what was real, Carla was unable to make choices that were good for her. Completing the vicious cycle was Carla's self-blame when things went badly.

Ben was surprised to learn that the pressure of all the things he hadn't said to Carla were part of what led him to the affair. When it came to talking about his feelings, he had been mute. Finally, he acted them out in a big way. A major issue for Ben was his shame at feeling jealous of his son, Adam. Ever since Adam's birth, Carla had paid much more attention to Adam than to Ben. Because of his shame, Ben had never told Carla of his pain at losing her attention. Now, with the help of a counselor, they were starting to uncover and share the burdens each had carried alone.

This work also helped them make sense of the affair. In short, because they didn't know how to connect with each other emotionally, Carla had turned to Adam, their son, for an emotional response, and Ben had turned to Janet. As Carla began to understand what happened she remarked, "I need to grow through this— I don't want to end up bitter."

You may be ready to identify how the two of you set the stage for an affair. To find out what's beneath the affair in your relationship, take some time to go through the following questions with your spouse.

How Did the Two of You Ever Get to This Place?

- What attracted you to your spouse in the very beginning?
- Were these positive characteristics still present when you got engaged?
- Were they still present when you got married?
- When did you first notice any changes in these aspects of your relationship?
- What else was going on around the time these changes occurred? (Pregnancy, the birth of a child, the death of a parent, a major promotion, winning the lottery, the loss of a job, a trauma . . .)

- How did the two of you address the events or the crisis you have identified? Did you talk about it? If so, what did you actually say to your partner? Did your words leave a lot unsaid?
- What happened in your relationship between that event or crisis and the beginning of the affair?
- What expectations did you have of your partner or your marriage that were unfulfilled? What did you actually say about those expectations to your partner?

Use the information from your discussion to come up with one or two sentences that describe what each of you contributed to setting the stage for an affair. Carla and Ben might say, "We both stopped talking to each other after Adam was born." Or it might sound like this: Carla: "I wasn't really aware of being down, and I certainly didn't want to be a nag like my mother, so I didn't say much." Ben: "I couldn't stand feeling so jealous so I tried not to be, but that just made things worse, and I ended up turning to Janet for some attention." Once you agree on what happened, you can identify the changes you need to make in your relationship.

If you find it's hard to talk, you can write down your answers to each question, and then share your responses to each question with each other. If you get stuck in this process, get professional help so that you can reach an understanding of how you got here.

Special Problems That Fuel Obsession

Moving beyond obsession is harder when your spouse is leaving the marriage, especially when your spouse is leaving to be with the third party. You are facing a double whammy: the betrayal and the marital separation. It will be hard to resist the temptation to blame it all on your spouse (or the third party). Doing that, however, would be a tragedy. Opportunities are often created out of painful circumstances. This is the time to learn to give yourself a voice and to grow rather than to make yourself a living monument to betrayal. Letting go of obsession is also more difficult when you have been married for a long time, particularly when you have sacrificed parts of yourself along the way. If you have put aside your needs for the good of your spouse or your marriage, you may have little self left. As you reclaim the lost parts of yourself and give them a voice, you will be able to let go of the obsession.

Affairs with a family friend or a spouse's best friend are not quite incest, but they feel close. Shock waves ripple through your support network when this happens. If you're the betraying spouse, it will be important to give up the idea that you can rebuild your marriage *and* continue the friendship. There are violations of friendship that go too deep to be rectified. It's hard enough to rebuild the marriage after this double betrayal. Even if your affair partner was not a family friend, you won't be able to continue the friendship if you want your marriage. (Affairs with family members are discussed in Chapter Ten.)

Many affairs are with a work colleague. Knowing that the spouse who betrayed you has daily contact with the third party makes it hard to believe that the affair has really ended. Yet many times it has. It's even harder when you have to have contact with the third party on a regular basis, as for example when that person answers the phone in your spouse's office. If your spouse really seems to have ended the affair and is working on the marriage, see if you can rise above the temptation to be cutting or sarcastic. Make yourself the class act. While it is not always possible or practical for your spouse to change jobs, it is something the two of you might seriously consider for business as well as personal reasons. Remember, the workplace too is tainted by an affair, affecting the perspective of others in the office toward all involved.

In a few cases the third party won't let go. There are phone calls, letters, or attempts to bump into the affair partner. Sometimes this means the affair is continuing, but in other situations it's because the third party is having difficulty giving up the affair. If your spouse is clear and firm about ending the affair, these contacts should end fairly soon. If they do not end, the affair is continuing or the third party is having difficulty with reality and may actually pose a danger to you or your spouse. If that is the case, see Chapter Four.

Summary

Think of obsession as a gateway for opening up your issues. Don't expect it to go away overnight, but by focusing on your real emotions and claiming your share of responsibility for the marital problems, you can gradually let go of the affair. As the obsession subsides, sadness at what's been lost takes its place alongside your other feelings. By the time the obsessing fades, you are on your way to rebuilding your life, either as an individual or as a couple.

Chapter Six

Working on the Marriage

Building a Sense of Trust and Belonging

> The previous chapter in your life has been written.
> What matters now is what you give birth to.

An affair is like the treetop that draws a lightning bolt. It is natural to pay more attention to the resulting fire than to what attracted the fire to this particular spot. But bystanders tend to fan these flames rather than help fight them, thus distracting you from understanding the conditions that ignited the fire and from taking steps to prevent future fires. You can use this trauma as a catalyst for turning your life around and maybe your marriage as well. It's an opportunity not to be wasted.

So now that you've gotten through the worst of the obsession about the affair, how *do* you go about rebuilding your life? Will you ever be able to trust again? Will your marriage survive? If it does, will you feel that bond of belonging that you crave? That you may once have experienced? How *do* you rebuild trust?

An affair doesn't have to mean your marriage is over. It does mean that there's no time to waste before getting to work on rebuilding your relationship on different terms. Learning how to talk straight about your uncomfortable feelings, how to resolve your differences, and how to negotiate between separate and together space are a few of the tasks that rebuild trust. The most difficult task is taking the risk of letting your real self be known by your partner.

Alternatively, you can choose not to do this work, but your marriage will be stagnant. It may have some good elements, but the safe and lonely distance between the two of you will grow. If you continue to use external things—new clothes or a new car, another party, or another trip—to feel alive, expect affairs to resurface.

In this chapter we will focus on how Conflict Avoiders and Intimacy Avoiders can go about bringing new life to their relationship. You don't have to know that the marriage will continue in order to do the necessary work, but you do need to have a solid commitment to work on rebuilding the marriage. For you to work together, the affair must be over—physically and emotionally. Rebuilding involves a commitment to work on specific behaviors and tasks for a minimum of three months, to rule out separation and divorce for now, and to continue in marital therapy. Expect the work to take considerably longer than three months, but by the end of three months you will know whether any changes are occurring. By doing the work you will find out whether you can make the marriage fit you both. If you don't know whether rebuilding is even an option, the next part of this chapter will help you assess your situation.

If the affair is the Sexual Addiction or Split Self type, you will need to work on healing your childhood wounds before you are ready to work on rebuilding trust with each other. In other words, you need first to get a handle on what is driving *you*. Turn to the next chapter, Chapter Seven, for guidance about healing old wounds. After your individual healing is under way, come back to this chapter for information on moving ahead as a couple. If the affair in your life is an Exit Affair, the option of working together on rebuilding your marriage isn't available. However, you still need to do much of the same work—but separately. See Chapter Eight for ideas on how this works.

Prerequisites for Rebuilding Trust

You're ready to work on rebuilding trust and healing your selves and your marriage when the following indicators are in place:

- The affair has been revealed.
- The affair has ended.

- Any ongoing contact between the affair partners, such as at work, is being handled openly and appropriately.
- The obsession, although not totally done with, has diminished.
- You still like and care about each other.
- You have a beginning sense of how the two of you made room for the affair.
- You are *both* committed to working on yourselves and on the marriage, knowing that it will be painful and will take longer than you want and that you have no guarantees of how it will all come out.

Untangling the Present from the Past

In marriage, your past and your spouse's past came together in ways that you didn't expect. Most of us unwittingly pick a partner who fits our own unfinished business. Then we play out this business in our marriage, hoping that this time we can satisfactorily resolve the problem—but without quite identifying the nature of that problem. It's this playing out of old issues that accounts for so much of the emotional withholding and the go-nowhere fighting in marriages. Michael describes this pattern in talking about his marriage: "My wife pulls the same old stuff my mother did. I realize now that either I trained her or I found a woman to marry who brought the tools to the job."

Here's how some of the old baggage played out for Jim and his wife, Vickie. Jim's father was depressed when Jim was a kid and not emotionally available. Jim still fears being emotionally abandoned by the important people in his life. He tries to accommodate to whatever he thinks Vickie wants so that she won't abandon him. Jim's behavior taps directly into Vickie's old baggage. As a child, Vickie experienced her mother's advice and efforts to help as smothering, but she was afraid her mother would fall apart if she didn't cooperate. Jim's efforts to please her feel similar, but she puts up with them silently, telling herself that she should be happy that he is so nice.

Jim and Vickie are Conflict Avoiders, with neither fully aware or talking about the discomforts and fears that are driving their behavior with each other. Vickie's affair is the culmination of Jim's and Vickie's unfinished business with their own parents. Even after the affair was out in the open, Jim's obsession had kept them both from having to come out of hiding. Now, he is beginning to see how afraid he has always been of being abandoned. He coped by staying in control, trying to fix this or that for Vickie, and never sharing his abandonment fears. Vickie's affair was an expression of her anger at Jim; anger that she was afraid to feel or give voice to.

Coupled with old baggage are misguided beliefs. Our culture pushes the idea that if your spouse loves you, you will feel whole—that your spouse will meet all your needs, whenever you want, just because you want them met. From this shaky perch it is an easy step to thinking, "If I don't feel whole, it must be my spouse's fault"—which makes it seem reasonable to look for someone who will make you feel whole. If you don't jettison this idea, you could spend your entire life moving from one partner to the next, looking for someone to make you feel like a whole person. Neither of you can make the other feel whole or resolve the other's old baggage. Each of you has responsibility for doing this yourself, even if you need therapy to make the shift. Making ourselves feel whole is the work of growing up. Fortunately, we can resume the work of growing up at any age.

The reality of old baggage and the myth of love's power have a lot to do with why one or both of you turned to an affair. Once you understand these concepts, you'll realize that an affair partner comes with old baggage too; and *it's always baggage that correlates with yours.* Thus an early task in rebuilding your marriage is to distinguish between old baggage and the real differences between the two of you. Baggage has to do with strategies you've developed to cope with (or avoid) pain, fear, or conflict. Real differences have to do with basic temperament, preferences, physical aptitudes, and communication styles (visual, auditory, or touch). You will need to learn how to bridge your real differences in ways that work for both of you. Awareness of your old baggage makes it easier to recognize and resolve your real differences.

"How Can I Ever Trust You Again?"

As you move out of crisis mode you venture into a period of exploration and change. It is time for the scary business of taking your thoughts and feelings out of your internal safety deposit box and sharing them with your partner. There is no healing without a willingness to risk again. If you want your marriage, you will need to make changes in how you interact with each other. Since you can't make your partner change, it comes down to making changes in yourself. However, one spouse can't rebuild the relationship alone. You've got a good chance of rebuilding a better relationship when you both can discuss the changes needed, dovetail them, hold yourselves accountable, and share your emotional ups and downs.

Trust is rebuilt by behavior, not by words. Rebuilding trust requires that each of you develop the skills of intimacy: paying attention to your emotions, being honest, giving yourself a voice, owning responsibility, becoming emotionally vulnerable, and developing reasonable expectations for your marriage. Shame and fear will be your biggest enemies.

It's easy to be in a relationship when things are going smoothly. Commitment is demonstrated by being present when the going gets hard.

Paying Attention to Your Emotions

Attempts to honor your own feelings are regarded as selfish in some families. Other families believe in keeping secret anything that might be embarrassing or painful. Still others avoid conflict, and family members who are angry are soothed or isolated or otherwise taught not to express or even pay attention to their own anger. Such a heritage makes it difficult to know what is real. Whatever the family pattern, each partner brings his or her own version of it to the marriage. Efforts to merge the two styles create additional stress.

To be honest with yourself, you need to know the difference between your thoughts and your feelings. Both your thoughts and your feelings are essential to giving yourself a voice, but first focus on your feelings. Check yourself out right now. What are you feeling? If you can express it as "I feel x," it is probably a feeling. If you start with "I feel that—" or if you start presenting the facts of the situation, you are not paying attention to your feelings. If you are having trouble knowing what you feel, scan your body. What are you experiencing in your physical self? What is your stomach feeling? Your neck and shoulders? Are you tapping your feet or your fingers? Is there any physical tension in your body? Is there any movement? Any pain? What other sensations do you notice in your physical self? Maybe you feel that something is stuck in your throat, or your stomach is churning, or your jaw hurts from grinding your teeth. Sometimes the physical sensation translates directly to your emotions, as when you notice, "I feel tense." In other cases, the physical symptom may be metaphorical, as for example, the stuck sensation in your throat when you are choking back your anger.

See if you can shift your focus from your physical to your emotional self. You might notice that you feel hurt, or scared, or furious, or all of these. *Stay away from thinking about why you feel this way or what you are going to do, and just feel whatever emotions are present.* As you stay with your feelings, notice how they ebb and flow. Your pattern may be to avoid certain feelings: especially pain, shame, or fear. Let yourself feel them. You won't be stuck with feeling something forever if you give the feeling its space. If you continue to have difficulty in knowing what you feel, consider seeing a counselor for help.

Remember that you were born with full access to your emotions, and you learned, for specific reasons, not to pay attention to them. This prevents you from being emotionally present with others. You can relearn how to access this very important part of yourself once again. Your emotions are critical, not only in being honest with your partner, but they are the very substance of connecting emotionally with any other person.

Being Honest

With an affair, dishonesty on the part of both spouses is the norm. The affair is an escalation of other dishonesties: the white lies, the hidden resentments, the less-than-honest excuses, and the denial of problems. Since the most troubling aspect of an affair is the dishonesty, rebuilding trust has to incorporate honesty. Trust depends on honesty in all matters, big and small—not just honesty about the affair. Any untruth raises questions about everything else you say. Dishonesty can be active or passive—information withheld can be as significant in destroying trust as is false information.

A lack of honesty can come from many sources. Did you learn early in life to sacrifice your own needs and feelings so as to protect someone else's feelings? Were you brought up to please others or to prevent conflicts, even if it meant distorting the truth? Did being honest mean getting punished or hit when you were a kid? Are you angry now but trying to hide it? Are you ashamed of what you feel? Did you learn as a kid to tune out your feelings because they were too painful? Did you learn how to be dishonest as a way of coping with situations that overwhelmed you or scared you as a child? Did you gain some power or control through omitting or distorting information? The basic question to ask yourself is, "What am I afraid will happen if I'm totally honest?"

Keep in mind that now that you're an adult you have more options than you did as a kid for coping with problem situations. Identify the old emotional baggage that has you feeling scared, powerless, or ashamed; tell your partner about it; then focus on how to solve the present issue on its own merits. For example, make your decision about buying a new car based on your needs and your finances rather than on meeting your parents' insistence on frugality or your desire to impress others or to counter your feelings of being powerless.

Learning to be honest with *yourself* is essential in this stage of the healing process after an affair. Being honest with your partner depends on being honest with yourself. What does this involve? What do you need to be honest about, you ask. The most common dishonesty is to decide that you will protect your partner from something you think or feel, because, after all, it is such a small matter, and you don't want to hurt your partner. Your dishonesty may stem from the fact that you don't want to deal with the possible consequences of your honesty. Your partner might not like what you have to say, may become angry, may push you away or punish you. When you get tired of suppressing so much of yourself, you may explode (so much for protecting your spouse!) or you may get depressed and become even more emotionally unavailable.

Affairs often form a smokescreen for still more unwelcome truths. Ed's affair resulted from his mismanagement of family finances coupled with Eileen's insistence that she not have to write checks or otherwise pay attention to money matters. When the financial jig was up and all the credit cards were maxed out with no money left for the house payment, Ed was still afraid to tell Eileen. Having an affair was an unconscious way of forcing the whole situation into view while, on the surface, honoring Eileen's desire to avoid dealing with finances.

Giving Yourself a Voice

With access to your emotions and honesty with yourself you are ready to work on learning key communication skills. The silent accommodations, the critical comments, and the reactive attacks need to be a thing of the past. Although their communication styles are different, Conflict Avoiders and Intimacy Avoiders need to work on the same thing: communicating in a way that works. Sexual Addicts and Split Selves also have this to learn, but they must do some individual work first.

Communicating effectively involves:

- Sending a clean and clear message.
- Transmitting your message in a manner that fits your spouse's listening style (presenting the information in large or small bites, keeping the discussion going or allowing a time-out for digesting the message, giving the bottom line first or starting with the details).
- Making sure your words and "music" (your feelings, body language) match.
- Starting your statements with "I".
- Knowing your spouse's vulnerabilities and choosing words that don't "hook" or "bait" your spouse.
- Inviting discussion rather than demanding or deciding for your spouse.
- Listening to your partner.
- Checking out your assumptions and interpretations.
- Staying on the main point.
- Acknowledging emotions.

An effective pattern of communicating is seen in the following discussion between Tom and Sheila, a young couple with dual careers and two kids under six.

> Tom: (*sends an "I" message about a specific problem*) I'm concerned that we don't seem to be able to find any time together.
>
> Sheila: (*listens, taking in the words and "music," repeats the message as she understands it, and asks if her interpretation is accurate*) You're concerned that we don't have time together. You sound angry about it too. Are you?
>
> Tom: (*responds to her question*) Yeah, I guess I am angry. (*asks about Sheila's concerns about the issue he has raised*) How do you feel about this?

Sheila: (gives an "I" message in response to Tom's question) I'm
concerned too. Right now it feels like I don't have any time
what with my job and the kids being sick. I am so tired that
sometimes I just want to run away from it all. I tell myself
this won't last, but I don't know how to make it different.
I'm discouraged.

Tom: (acknowledges Sheila's feelings) I know you're tired. *(suggests
an option for resolving the problem)* I am too, but I think if we
can find a way to spend some time together we might be able
to relax a bit.

Sheila: (expresses her doubts about her ability to use that option)
I don't know what I can give up to make time. I've got to go
to work and the kids have to be taken care of. By then it's
10 P.M. and I'm exhausted.

Tom: (proposes a brief brainstorming session) If you're game, let's
take ten minutes just to shake loose some ideas about what
we might be able to do.

Sheila: (negotiates her terms for the brainstorming session) OK, if we
can talk as soon as the kids are in bed, and if it goes beyond
ten minutes, I want to stop and come back to it tomorrow.

Tom: (agrees to the terms) OK, it's a deal.

The important parts of this approach are the "I" statements,
staying on the issue while listening and responding, negotiating
terms, and avoiding attacks, even though both Tom and Sheila are
tired and Tom is angry as well. "I" messages are not selfish; they are
generous—they let your partner in on what's really going on inside
of you. You're sharing you, not just your facade. (You can't connect
emotionally with a facade!) Sharing *you* is how intimacy is built.

When the words and the music don't match it's tempting to
take the part you like and ignore the rest. Or if you're in a bad
mood, you may do just the opposite and stir up a fight. Sheila heard
Tom's mixed message (he voiced concern but the "music" indicated
he was angry) and checked it out. Sending a single message reduces
the possibility of this happening. A run-on message that states the

problem but then explains it, justifies it, and adds extraneous details ends up being clutter. It's easy for the receiver to get lost in the detail or miss the main point.

Some spouses believe that a partner who really cares should simply *know* what's wrong. Moreover, they believe that their spouse should fix it without any input from them. Since most people are very poor at mind-reading this strategy doesn't work well. Intimacy Avoiders escalate this situation into a fight; Conflict Avoiders pretend there's not really a problem.

Other spouses believe that if they yell and describe their partner's "sins," they are expressing anger. This isn't an expression of anger; it's an attack. An attack may demonstrate that you're angry but it doesn't tell your mate what's going on inside you. The attack focuses on what the other has done wrong rather than how you feel. Your partner will probably try to guess what's going on with you but will eventually get tired and tune you out. Anger can be expressed without attacking. In fact an attack is a poor way of expressing anger because it often triggers the "fight or flight" syndrome, where the other person becomes defensive and stops listening, either distancing or attacking back. When the fight pattern is activated, anger can rapidly escalate into a nasty struggle. In the early stages, anger can often be defused by simply acknowledging it, as Sheila did with Tom.

If you're angry, you can say, "I'm angry at 'x'"—and no more. Give your partner a chance to respond. See if you can talk the problem through using a dialogue like that between Tom and Sheila. If anger continues to be a problem, you might read *The Dance of Anger* by Harriet Goldhor Lerner.[1] If you fear that your anger will make you lose control, or if sometimes you're afraid of your partner's anger, read Chapter Four on preventing violence. If anger leads to rage or loss of control, you need professional help.

Additional guidelines for giving yourself a voice when communicating with your partner include the following:

- Pay attention to your own internal warning system and your own feelings.

- Share your emotions with your spouse, preferably at the moment when something is happening between you; otherwise as soon as possible at a time that works for both of you.

- When you feel irritated or uncomfortable, look inside for feelings of being trapped, smothered, hurt, or scared.

- Voice your irritation, annoyance, or discomfort as soon as you are aware of it.

- Use "I" statements to express what you are thinking and feeling.

- Listen to your spouse without prejudging.

- Stay in the present. Leave out the history of who did what to whom.

- Remember that feeling angry (or feeling any other emotion) doesn't mean you have to act it out. You have many choices about how to handle what you are feeling.

- If you find yourself attacking or being attacked, change gears—and if that doesn't work, take a time-out and get some distance from each other, returning to the real issues later when you are both able to listen and to talk.

- Get to know each other by voluntarily disclosing your thoughts and feelings and by inviting and listening to your spouse's thoughts and feelings.

Owning Responsibility

Taking responsibility for yourself and your choices is a significant issue in all types of affairs. It has to do with the choices you make and with holding yourself accountable for your actions. Prior to and during an affair your attention and that of your spouse has been anywhere but on taking responsibility for yourselves. If you're a Conflict Avoider, you've probably been focused on not rocking the boat; on keeping things going smoothly despite your feelings of dissatisfaction and your guilt about the affair. When you're an Intimacy Avoider, you're more likely to have focused on protecting yourself from being trapped, through fighting, humor, or other means of keeping a distance.

Boundary Drift. One element of responsibility is setting and respecting boundaries. Limits and boundaries can be changed, but not without communication. This idea of boundaries applies in all human relationships, including marriage.

With affairs, *boundary drift* is always part of the picture. It occurs when you get into the habit of letting yourself or your partner slide across a boundary without comment. Most boundary violations are small matters. For example, saying you'll be home at 7:30 but arriving at 8:15 without calling is a boundary violation. So is spending much more than the agreed-upon amount for a new winter coat. Hiding the amount spent is another boundary violation. Boundary drift is a combination of the violation and the absence of attempts by either spouse to address it. You drift along, not taking responsibility for yourself and not holding your partner accountable. You may even put up with behavior that is hurtful or engage in behavior that results in your feeling guilty or ashamed. The dead space that develops between you and your partner when you don't act responsibly or talk honestly provides plenty of room for boundary drift. The small incursions grow into big advances. An affair is often the result.

Boundary drift occurs in your head before it occurs in reality. Larry is talking about boundary drift as he explains how he moved toward his affair, "I was doing everything I could to let it happen, but I didn't want the responsibility for its happening." Caroline describes placing an old boyfriend into her image of the ideal partner: "I reached into my past and conjured him into my present."

Becoming Aware of Your Responsibility Issues. Avoiding responsibility is a way of trying to get what you want without paying the price. You'll need to give up the fantasy of discovering the perfect partner who will provide you with everything you want. It won't happen—and you don't need it anyway. Letting go of the hope that someone else will take care of you is difficult, but meeting the challenge of taking responsibility for yourself can be very satisfying. Moreover, it doesn't leave you dependent on finding a fantasy creature to fill your needs.

Being conscious of what you are doing and the choices you are making is the first step in being responsible. Second is holding yourself accountable for your choices and your behavior. You'll probably have to face some things about yourself that you don't like, such as admitting to yourself your less than desirable motives and behaviors. Note each time you duck an issue, and explore your fear of tackling it. One man noted that when he put emotional constraints on himself regarding little pleasures, he exploded later with a big purchase. He realized a similar pattern with his affair. He'd been upset but held it back from his wife, saying instead, "Whatever you want, dear." Then he had an affair.

To get a sense of what you might do to act more responsibly, ask yourself: When you were growing up, how would you have wanted your father or mother to behave if they were in the same situation you are in? Would you have wanted them to talk to each other? To stop lying to one another? To stop disappearing? To talk to you? To get help? Your answer probably has to do with wanting your parents to behave in a more responsible manner. Use your answers to guide your own behavior.

Holding your partner accountable for commitments made to you is another aspect of being responsible. This does not mean being your partner's watchdog. Rather it means speaking up when you have a concern, rather than letting things slide. Speaking up does not mean your partner has to do what you want. However, if you're giving voice to your perspective rather than demanding your partner take care of you, chances are good that your partner will take you seriously and you will be able to talk the issue through.

Bill, who has avoided conflict throughout his marriage, got his courage together and brought up a long-standing problem: "You keep telling me that you're going to take care of filing the insurance forms, but it doesn't seem to get done until I nag you about it, and then you resent me. I don't understand why it's such a problem." Betsy responded, "I *am* going to get it done; I just haven't had time." Bill came back to his point, "It keeps being a problem. I don't want to nag you. Let's talk about what's going on that it keeps being a problem." Bill is gently but persistently holding Betsy accountable, while indicating he's open for a different kind of discussion of the issue. His concern is filing the insurance forms, not that Betsy must take care of them.

Becoming Emotionally Vulnerable

The affair doesn't mean that your ability to love and care are gone; they were only overshadowed by your pain, your fears, and your loneliness. You or your partner were looking outside your relationship for what you didn't know how to find or recapture inside. Thus an important part of rebuilding is looking inward at your self and at your marriage. What were your past expectations for your marriage? How can you make more realistic assessments and find ways to deal with disappointments? Can you increase your ability to see your own limitations? For those who fear intimacy, can you care and let your caring be seen? For those who fear conflict, can you expose your less agreeable self?

Speaking up about your emotional self is scary. It takes away your protective covering and you become emotionally vulnerable. Maybe your spouse won't like the real you. Or maybe you'll have to give up an advantage you've maintained by hiding out. Your hiding place will be gone as well. Perhaps you'll feel trapped. On the positive side, exposing your real and vulnerable self is how you rebuild trust. In giving up self-protection, a kind of defensive power, you gain the power of feeling like a grown-up, in charge of your own life.

Start small—even smaller if you're an Intimacy Avoider. Take selected emotional risks with your partner. Casey's usual style is to pretend she's got everything under control. She decided to take the risk of talking to Matt about her sense of hopelessness at work. Matt at first thought Casey wanted him to "fix" her feelings and tried to cheer her up. This irritated Casey but she kept her cool and told him she didn't want him to fix it, she just needed him to hear how down she was. After Matt relaxed and listened he responded, "Yeah, I feel like that sometimes too, and it's terrible." Casey's risk resulted in emotional support from Matt, rather than the put-down she feared. This kind of self-disclosure is one of the building blocks of intimacy.

Developing Reasonable Expectations for Your Marriage

Intimacy doesn't mean constantly being with your partner. It means connecting emotionally, being present with your spouse in the moment. Of course, that isn't possible all the time. Real life has other tasks that require practical discussions, caring for the kids, household chores, work responsibilities, errands, and the like. In addition, you each need time for yourself and time with the family, friends, and activities that you value. Thus it's essential to know how to move closer and how to move apart without using an affair to do so. Tell your partner when you need some physical or emotional space, negotiate the timing when you can, and let your spouse know when you'll be available again. If you find yourself mounting an attack or disappearing when you need space, examine your old baggage about power and control, and work on being honest and giving yourself a voice about the space you need.

It's OK for partners to have different preferences and different needs. If you pay attention to them and discuss them, you can work out arrangements that suit you both. You won't find a perfect match, and each of you will be disappointed on occasion. If you have difficulty handling your disappointment, or if the two of you get into power struggles over your differences, you need to work on constructive ways to take care of *yourself* when things don't go as you want or expect. Learning that you can handle and live with life's disappointments is an important part of growing up.

A serious power imbalance is present if one spouse makes all the important decisions, or if one generally accommodates so the other won't get upset. This indicates an unwillingness or a fear of being vulnerable. You can't have an intimate relationship with this kind of power imbalance. Giving up some of your control in order to share power with your spouse will feel risky. Claiming your power will feel equally risky.

Expect your rebuilding process to have its ups and downs. It takes tremendous energy and concentration to change entrenched habits. You will slip at times—when you do, own up and get yourself back on track. Your rebuilding process will take longer than you want and you will become impatient on occasion. Change takes time—let yourself take that time without passing judgment on yourself or your spouse for needing the time. Be aware that in learning how to change your behavior, you are developing a skill that will be valuable in the years ahead.

Healthy relationships grow and change. Therefore, you have to continually update your ways of expressing yourselves. When you find that a particular approach isn't working, give the problem some joint attention. Rick, for example, used humor for years, but it became annoying to Sara. Rick was shocked and hurt by the change in Sara, since he'd always used humor to take the sting out of things. With Sara's encouragement, he began to tell her how he really felt at those times. Sara readily acknowledged Rick's hurt, and let him know that she felt much closer to him when he let her in like this.

Resolving Remaining Issues Around the Affair

After your rebuilding is well under way, it's time to take another look at the affair to see what leftovers remain. Lingering questions related to the affair are probably tied to deeper aspects of how and why the affair occurred. Strong reactions at this point suggest that old baggage is the culprit. For example, June's obsession with trust kept coming back and when it did, she again questioned Dan about his affair. Hidden was her difficulty with trust that dated back to childhood when her mother periodically humiliated her with criticism. The deeper aspect for June was that she was just plain afraid to trust. Her search for answers was an attempt to find a risk-free way to have an intimate marriage—an impossibility. She was faced with deciding whether to be in touch with her deeper fears (and be vulnerable) or stay safe (and be alone). Once she understood this, she chose to take some very small risks and gradually learned to open herself up to Dan.

Sometimes the leftover issue is sadness at giving up the early idealism you shared; sadness at letting go of your dreams of the perfect future together. Letting go of your dreams hurts, but it frees you to move on to new dreams—dreams that are based on reality and that are a better fit for who you are today.

When Your Marriage Doesn't Make It

Sometimes, no matter how hard you work on your marriage, you come to the point of realizing that it's not going to work. Perhaps what drew you together was your old baggage—and without it you don't have the emotional bond that's needed. Or maybe you've grown in such different directions that you have little in common. Or possibly you have outgrown a spouse who has chosen not to change.

A decision to end your marriage that is made after serious work on your relationship is much different from an impulsive decision made upon learning of the affair. Sadness is the dominant emotion in this situation, not anger. There's no rush to flee. Instead you shift from working on your marriage to considering how to end it in as amicable a way as possible. Because of the work you've done, friendship may be a real possibility in the future. Chapter Eight describes the emotional steps in rebuilding your life after separation and divorce.

Summary

Rebuilding your relationship means growing emotionally. Honesty with your partner and with yourself is essential. Real honesty requires paying attention to what you are feeling as well as what you are thinking. Trust in yourself depends on taking responsibility for your own decisions and behavior. This combination enables you to approach problems in an adult manner and to risk emotional intimacy with your partner. These skills of intimacy are the tools that protect your future. While there are no guarantees against future affairs, the probability is low when two grown-ups stay current and are committed to the time, energy, and hard work that a high-quality marriage takes.

Chapter Seven

Working on Your Self

Healing Childhood Wounds

*Dressing, closing, and regularly tending to your
wounds is the beginning of nurturing yourself.*

The previous chapter addressed the issues that Conflict Avoiders
and Intimacy Avoiders face in rebuilding their marriages. This
chapter speaks to Sexual Addicts and Split Selves about healing
their deep childhood wounds, the aftereffects of which continue to
obstruct their lives and their relationships.

For Sexual Addicts and Split Selves, the first order of business
following an affair is not work on your marriage but work on yourself. This is true for both the betraying spouse, who in these affairs
is most often a man, and for the betrayed spouse. If there's to be
work on the marriage, the bulk of it comes later, after the individual work is well along.

Although Split Selves and Sexual Addicts have lived their
lives in almost opposite ways, the roots of both types of affairs lie
buried in early wounds. The use, abuse, and neglect of the past
needs to be addressed by each spouse head-on, rather than trying
to buy relief by taking care of others, acting out fantasies, or med-
icating oneself with sex. Deciding which is the right partner, finding one more person to have sex with, or trying to change your
spouse's behavior hasn't healed these wounds yet. Your focus needs
to be on paying attention to your own wounds and how they are
disabling you. The problem is internal and the inside of you needs
to be the focus of your work. Until your healing process is under
way, neither of you will be able to fully participate in working with

your spouse on the marriage. Later on this individual work can provide a solid base for sorting out your marriage.

First we will explore issues that the betraying spouse in a Split Self Affair needs to address; then the issues for the betrayed spouse. Next the issues facing the Sexual Addict will be addressed, followed by issues for the spouse of the Sexual Addict. Keep in mind that the family background and the childhood wounds are similar for both spouses in a Split Self Affair. Likewise, Sexual Addicts and their spouses share similar backgrounds and comparable wounds (though different backgrounds and wounds from those of the Split Selves).

Split Self Affairs

Split Selves are rational and responsible—overly so. Early in life they learned that their job was to attend to the needs of others and not to their own needs and feelings. Thus they approach life using only their rational self—a rational self that is not informed by the emotional self. This is the internal split that needs to be healed. Much of the initial work for both spouses is devoted to getting acquainted with the emotional self. For the betraying spouse, this work usually precedes making any decision about the marriage or the affair.

When You Are the Betraying Spouse in a Split Self Affair

You can't work on your marriage until you've ended your affair. You won't be able to end your affair, emotionally as well as physically, until you work on yourself. Understanding and healing your internal split is your first order of business. That internal split doesn't mean you have a multiple personality. It means you're pulled in two different directions. Your internal split plays out as trying to please—or avoid displeasing—your wife (who seems awfully like your mother these days), while pursuing a passionate emotional connection with your affair partner (you feel like you're coming alive in the affair). One part of you is focused on taking care of others, another part focuses on your needs, and between these two parts of you is a wall.

Split Selves learned early to put the needs of others first. In childhood it was a parent's needs that had to be honored; as an adult it is the needs of your spouse and your children, and maybe your colleagues too. You perceive attending to your own needs as selfish. As a child it may have been impossible to get your needs met because one or both of your parents was too needy, too angry, or too sick. You never had the kind of emotional connection with your parents that kids should have. You learned to bite your tongue, stay out of harm's way, and to please (or avoid displeasing) those around you. Roger, whose father was an alcoholic, learned early to tiptoe so that he didn't set off another rage or drinking binge. He observed, "I lived the first part of my life for my parents, the second part for my job and my family, and now I want some time for myself!"

Growing up you told yourself that you would do things differently from your parents—and you probably have. However what you've gotten good at is deciding what other people need and trying to give it to them, rather than saying how you feel—just the opposite of the skills you need for a strong relationship.

When you got married you vowed again, "My marriage isn't going to be like my parents'—I'm going to do this right." So you tried to build the perfect structure. You overlooked and put aside any disappointments so they didn't spoil your perfect scenario. Daily life kicked in, especially after the kids arrived, and reality spoiled the illusion of perfection. Your marriage isn't making you feel good the way it's supposed to. You put aside your disappointment and buckle down to doing what needs to be done. Maybe if you work harder, your spouse will be more loving. You're so busy trying to take care of your spouse and your kids that you don't have close friends that you can really talk with.

You long to be loved, but you still believe it depends on being good. Your rational self is overdeveloped and your emotional self is underdeveloped. Your feelings are buried—you don't tune in to your pain or your fear—instead you try to compute what will satisfy your spouse. You get more and more depressed. Meanwhile, in another corner of your mind, is the desire to be swept up, to be overpowered with love, to be in a warm womblike nest with everything provided, to have someone make you feel whole. You tell yourself that your day will come as a result of doing the right thing. Your day keeps being deferred as you take care of everyone else's needs. You're primed for an affair.

Feeling Fed Up! You're tired of being responsible for everyone else, but you don't say so—you don't want to hurt your spouse's feelings, and besides you don't know what you would say. Since you're doing everything you can to satisfy your spouse and it is not working, it must be your spouse's fault—if only your spouse would just do things right!

You picked a spouse you thought would give you the mothering you missed. You and she have been mother and father to each other, more than husband and wife. Now you're looking for something other than mothering. You're tired of the advice that comes with the mothering. You're fed up with taking care of others and deferring your own needs. You're ready to move on to another phase of life. You don't say so, nor do you start paying attention to your needs—you don't know how. Then along comes a woman who takes the time to listen to you, who tells you you're wonderful, who cares about how you feel, who speaks to your fantasies. The Other Woman dances into the lonely space inside you. She feeds your fantasy of being swept up by the perfect woman who will love you and make you feel whole. (You feed her fantasies as well.) After all the missed connections in your life, she is irresistible and you get seriously involved.

You struggle to understand the meaning of your affair. Your rational mind views it as a matter of deciding between your wife and your lover. Over and over again you ask yourself, "Which woman is the right woman for me? What is the right decision?"

Shifting gears to a different way of looking at your situation is difficult because you prefer thinking to feeling. "Everything under control," is your theme. Pain? Powerlessness? Not you! You're in control, although your wife would describe you as wimping out.

Part of why you're stuck is your reliance on your rational self. You see your problems as external and look for external solutions to them. However, your words and your "music" don't match. Here's how the pattern may be playing out:

Split Selves—Outside and Inside

Outside View	Rational Barrier	Subterranean Self
Agreeable	Depressed	Fed up
Accommodating	Guilty	Angry
In control	Ambivalent	Vulnerable
	Confused	Passionate
		Hurting
		Powerless

You do have another side—the self that can feel passionate, excited—and vulnerable. It is this little-known part of you that the affair has tapped into. You still don't know that these feelings are a part of *you*—you believe that these wonderful feelings result when the Other Woman waves her magic wand and sprinkles passion dust over you. She has become your lifeline to the world of feelings. You rely on her to provide the excitement, the newness, the passion in your life—you want these emotions in your everyday life—but you still rely on your spouse for a sense of family.

From Passion to Double Bind. Over time, the situation evolves into a double bind. Both your spouse and your affair partner expect your time and attention. You're still trying to make the right decision. This was Doug's situation. "I just need to make a decision," he announced. "You see, I've been seeing this woman for two years now, and I really love her, but I can't seem to get up the courage to leave my wife. I don't understand why it's so difficult!"

Doug, forty-six, and Janie, forty-four, have been married for twenty-two years. Janie learned of Doug's affair with Karen a year ago when she found a mushy greeting card addressed to Karen in Doug's briefcase. Doug moved out for two weeks, then moved back in saying he wanted to make the marriage work. However he is still seeing Karen, which Janie alternately ignores and rages against. Karen is twenty-nine, single, and works for the same company as Doug. She sees herself as the ideal partner for Doug and wonders why he stays with Janie since Janie obviously hasn't kept up with Doug—she's not interested in his work, or even in her own appearance. Karen has been pushing Doug recently to get up the courage to tell Janie that he is moving out.

Janie feels distraught. She can't believe that Doug has done this to her, especially after all her sacrifices for him. She can't sleep, she's lost eight pounds in the past month, and she is putting what little energy she has into trying to make herself physically and sexually attractive to Doug.

Doug keeps trying to make a decision: "I just need to figure out which is the right way to go." He talks about how important his family is to him, about not wanting to hurt his kids or to hurt Janie, but says, "I'm in love with Karen. I feel good with her—with her it's easy." Karen is emotionally present in a way that Janie is not, and Doug has tuned in to that presence.

Janie wants the marriage to work even though she is furious and doesn't know if she can ever forgive Doug. Janie sees herself as "nice" and is not direct with her anger. Doug says that he doesn't know if they can make it work; he cares about Janie, but, well he just isn't sure. . . . He is continuing to see Karen.

What is going on here? Why can't Doug either get it together or at the very least, just move out and give Janie some peace? Actually Doug is trying the only way he knows how to get his emotional needs met. He is following in his parents' martyr-like footsteps—a classic "nice guy" who stays busy doing things for everyone else but who doesn't share his emotional self. He doesn't pay attention to what he is feeling, so he misses those internal red flags that would tell him he needs to do something about his personal and marital dissatisfactions. He was a sitting duck for an affair. His choice was a single woman who elicits his caretaking behavior and who, because she is emotionally present, arouses his passion. The knowledge that he can feel passion is brand new and he finds it irresistible.

Integrating Heart and Mind. If you're like Doug, you're probably thinking, "All I need to do is make a decision—it doesn't make sense to get into all this other psychological stuff." It's difficult to shift from rational analysis to your emotional self but all that analysis hasn't paid off yet. You will have to use your emotional self for anything to change. When you've grown up enough not to need a mother any more, you can risk not being a "good boy." An affair certainly breaks the "good boy" mold. These affairs are akin to late adolescence when teens break their parents' rules as part of learning about how to live their own lives in the larger world.

You've learned from the affair that passion is possible for you. What the affair doesn't do is help you integrate the two halves of yourself: the rational, do-it-right part and the self that has needs and feelings. Your work is to bring the two halves of you together. This requires paying attention to *your* feelings instead of everyone else's.

Your emotions are alien territory. The passion you experience with the Other Woman feels wonderful, but you don't know what to do with all those other feelings that are beginning to emerge. Suppressing the uncomfortable has been second nature to you since childhood. Now is the time to learn how to pay attention to your emotions, especially those that are uncomfortable. Professional help will be important in helping you learn about your emotional self.

Your first step in a new direction is to allow your self to feel fed up with trying to meet everyone's demands. Feeling fed up is crucial—it provides the motivation to change. Feeling fed up means a self is emerging; one with needs and feelings that have been denied and put aside for years. Your affair was an attempt to meet these needs, but it evolved into meeting still another person's demands. You won't be able to address *your* needs and feelings until you take them seriously and give yourself a voice. That's different from "making a decision," and much harder, but the rewards of feeling grown-up are great.

Close to feeling fed up is feeling powerless or helpless. These feelings are difficult for you because they are the opposite of being in control. Yet sometimes you are, in fact, powerless. Your typical pattern is to fight these feelings by making a decision, taking action, fixing things, staying busy, or finding someone to take care of. You distract yourself, but get no relief.

You can learn to tolerate feeling helpless or powerless by taking the following steps:

- Pay attention to your feelings of powerlessness. When you shift out of rational mode and tune in fully to your helpless feelings, you will experience some relief.

- Stay with your feelings of powerlessness. Don't distract yourself. This won't work if you *think* about feeling powerless—it only works if you let yourself *feel* powerless.

- Acknowledge the pain and disappointment that comes with feeling helpless.

- Accept your feelings of powerlessness. This means you realize that, at the moment, *there is nothing you can do.* (Try saying it out loud to yourself: *There is nothing I can do right now.*) You don't have to scramble around trying to fix and to do. You can just sit back and experience some temporary relief.
  You will find that your feelings of powerlessness recede after they've been given their due.

Healing Childhood Wounds. You've probably tuned out or rationalized the emotional content of your childhood experience. You'll need to go through a period of exploring and healing the residual pain stemming from childhood wounds. You can expect to feel angry, hurt, sad, terrified, helpless, relieved, amazed, and all sorts of other feelings. It will be a slow process, and you will need professional help. Painful as it is, this process will help you shed your underlying depression and feel more alive. When you don't have to stifle your emotions, they become available to you and enrich your life. Your emotions are the channel through which you can connect with others on an intimate level.

Do you remember, for example, the first time you felt ashamed in front of your friends or your parents? Did you have anyone you could talk to about what happened? How did you resolve your shame? Probably you buried it. Incidents like that teach you to suppress your awful feelings and to try to do things right. Now as an adult, you can risk exploring painful events such as this so that they no longer weigh you down.

In the process of facing and healing your childhood wounds, you will learn how to pay attention to your emotions. That gives you the base to begin working on the other skills of intimacy: becoming honest, giving yourself a voice, taking responsibility for yourself, and allowing yourself to be vulnerable with those you care about.

Taking responsibility for yourself can be particularly difficult, because it means giving up the fantasy that someone else will take care of you in the way you want. When you didn't get enough nurturing and attention as a child, it is very painful to give up the hope of finding that attention. Instead you looked for a partner who would make up for that early loss. However, you have an adult self now and can nurture yourself in a way you couldn't as a child.

Here is a technique for nurturing the vulnerable child that each of us carries inside. This young self is an innocent, uncontaminated, and emotional part of us. Because you learned that you should not pursue your own needs, or maybe also because you feared being too vulnerable, you buried this part of yourself long ago. You need to reclaim this child inside, and learn how to listen and to consult with this innermost part of you.

Use this technique to get to the down-deep innocent part of yourself.

Self-Nurturing Exercise

Close your eyes. Let your mind come up with pictures of your young self, around the ages of four, five, or six. Select an image that you like. Look at old photos of yourself if you are having difficulty finding an image that fits. Later on, when you are in deep pain or when your "button" has been pushed, let yourself shift to a mental image of this young self. Feel what that young part of yourself is experiencing right now. Is this young self frightened? Or hurt? It's important to let yourself go to this deeper level of pain or fear. While you stay with those feelings, identify what that part of you needs right now. Is it comfort of some sort? A kind word? A hug? Reassurance? Whatever it is, let your adult self give that child inside you what you need.

Steve, who is involved in a Split Self Affair, used this technique when he found himself fuming about all the demands being made on him. He was scared but wasn't in touch with feeling scared, only angry. When he visualized his five-year-old self and reached for his five-year-old's feelings, he started to cry. His five-year-old self felt scared—scared of being abandoned; afraid that his kids had no use for him now; scared that Nora, his affair partner, would leave him. This fear of being abandoned had haunted Steve all his life and was at the root of his problems with trust. Steve closed his eyes and envisaged his adult self hugging his five-year-old self. When he was actually five and scared, he had no one to comfort him. Now he has an adult self that can nurture the child inside.

You can also consult with your inner child to get a more accurate reading on your feelings when your rational self has you confused. Sometimes your inner child will have good ideas about what you need for healing. Remember that your inner child is not a vengeful child but an innocent child and needs to be protected in a way that he or she never has been.

Taking Responsibility for Yourself. Taking care of yourself also means being honest with yourself and others. No more untruths or "sins of omission." No trying to save your partner from feeling bad, so as to protect yourself from her displeasure. Your sense of personal integrity will grow as you speak up for yourself. Sometimes this will feel risky, because there's no guarantee that the other person will see it your way. But you don't really need to please others when you know that you can take care of yourself.

The other side of taking care of yourself is holding your partner accountable for her behavior. Rather than picking up the pieces your partner has dropped, expect your partner to pick up after herself. Also be less willing to put up with behavior that is hurtful or demeaning.

That doesn't mean you isolate yourself. Much the contrary. Not taking responsibility for how the other person feels frees you to be fully yourself. You will find that you can be more empathic when your partner is upset, and more compassionate with your partner's hurts. When you had to prevent your partner from feeling bad, or fix your partner's feelings, you were too busy with damage control to be compassionate.

The skills of intimacy, which are similar to the skills needed to care for oneself, are described in Chapter Six. As you learn to take good care of yourself emotionally you'll find that you no longer need a partner who will heal all your wounds. It's enough to find a partner who is in a similar process of taking care of herself.

When You Are the Betrayed Spouse in a Split Self Affair

First you don't want to see his affair. He makes sure you do, although he does it indirectly, through hotel charges on your MasterCard, the silk panties in his suitcase after a business trip (and he expects you to do his laundry!), or the love note stashed under the front seat of the car. Then you don't want to believe it's serious. He lets you know it is by repeatedly staying out to 1 or 2 A.M. and telling you he loves her. Oh, he loves you too, but he's in love with her. This is the missing romance that's slipped away from you. Next you try to persuade him that he's hurting the kids. He keeps agreeing with you but he misses half the kids' games and doesn't take them fishing anymore.

Developing a Backbone. You feel desperate and powerless, and your self-esteem, not great anyway, plummets. You rant and rave one minute, hoping that guilt will make him see how wrong he is. Twenty minutes later you accommodate his behavior or cover for him, hoping to win him back. The turning point comes when you finally realize you can't make your spouse change course, you can't hide it any longer from your kids or anyone else, and you're fed up with being the good girl and putting up with having his affair shoved in your face.

Janie, who has been learning to pay attention to her emotions, declared, "I've been responsible for everyone since I was three years old! I'm sick of it! I thought when I got married that somebody was finally going to take care of me! And here I am, still being responsible for everyone else! Well, those days are over!" Janie is starting to develop a backbone!

When you get to this point you can start setting some limits. It may be the first time in your life that you set limits. Setting limits will feel risky, but you're at risk anyway. Identify what you are no longer willing to put up with. Some possibilities for change include insisting that your spouse move out of your bedroom or even that he move out of the house as long as the affair is continuing. You might stop covering for him with his parents and with your kids. That does not mean dumping everything on your kids—it means saying, "Ask your father," instead of, "I'm sure he's working late." It may mean starting to take an active role in learning about family finances. It means beefing up your support system and making use of it. If he's out of the house and wants to move back in, it could mean insisting that the affair end and that you both get into therapy before you decide whether to let him move back in.

Getting Professional Help. It is just as important for you as for your spouse to get the professional help you need. Your background is much like your spouse's. You too are split internally, neglecting your own feelings and needs for much the same reasons as he.

Instead of having an affair, however, you've probably devoted yourself to your children, maybe to the extent that your husband felt crowded out of your life. You need to do the same work as he, learning to pay attention to your feelings and to voice them, and getting to work on healing your childhood wounds. Much of the work outlined for the betraying spouse earlier in this chapter will be equally useful for you.

Sometimes the wound is to one's sexual self. Such wounds come from overly sexualized behavior toward you or from sexual abuse when growing up. Janie was leery of her grandfather, who lived with her family, because he touched her breasts whenever he could get away with it and he would slip sexual innuendoes into his conversations with her. She shut off sexually to protect herself. She found it very difficult to enjoy sex in her marriage and avoided it when she could. Addressing this issue was an essential element of Janie's healing.

The Road Ahead

If you, the betraying spouse, have any thoughts of working on your marriage, you will need to end your affair. Sometimes ending the affair helps you work on yourself as well. Doug was beginning to understand that his internal split was really about denying his own feelings and performing for others in the hope they would care for him. He decided to end his affair when he saw that Janie was finally addressing her issues, issues that he had despaired would ever be addressed. She was learning to be emotionally present, just as Doug was. A second factor in his decision was his desire to be present in his children's lives on a daily basis. He missed the passion of the affair, but he felt hopeful that the changes he and Janie were making would lead to a more satisfying marriage in the future.

Doug's lingering emotional attachment to the third party is common when a Split Self Affair ends. It recedes as you take on responsibility for making your own life what you want it to be and don't need someone else to do it for you.

Alternatively, you may decide that you want the affair to continue, either parallel to the marriage or instead of the marriage. Continuing the marriage and the affair may mean that you're not ready to decide, or it may mean that you've decided, at least for now, to keep both relationships in your life. It's also possible that if you've been healing your wounds and generally working on yourself, and your spouse has not, you may have outgrown your marriage. You can only make a solid decision by paying attention to your emotions and taking responsibility for yourself, not by trying to please others or doing "the right thing."

Assessing Your Marriage. When you have moved along in resolving your old wounds and learned to pay attention to your needs and feelings, it's time for each of you to look again at your marriage. In answering the following questions you will get a sense of whether working on your marriage is a viable possibility.

- If the affair has ended, are you thinking that you would like your marriage to continue, or is the marriage such a shell that you don't want to continue with it?
- Do you like your spouse as a person?
- What characteristics of your spouse do you like?
- Is your spouse also working on healing old wounds and changing old patterns of behavior?
- Are you and your spouse emotionally present with each other?
- What between you is not working?
- What would need to change?
- Can you both commit to working on the necessary changes?
- Do you and your spouse have what it takes to work toward intimacy?
- Are you ready for a partner who is an adult?
- What do you want now in a partner?

Companionship and coupleship are the foundation of marriage. If you want the marriage, don't assume you can make it work if your spouse is not carrying his or her own responsibility for actively working on it. That's the old caretaking role you assumed in the past. It didn't work then, and it won't work any better now.

Making Decisions About Your Marriage. For those who decide to work on the marriage, sharing your pain about what has happened to your marriage is an important early step. A major piece of work throughout the rebuilding process is learning how to tolerate anxiety and powerlessness without taking control. The skills of intimacy described in Chapter Six will also be essential building blocks for your relationship.

Another possibility is that one or the other of you will decide that it is time to end your marriage. In Split Self Affairs, when this decision is a firm one, it usually follows the work of healing old wounds and developing the skills of intimacy. It may be that only one of you did the necessary work, or in doing the work you found you did not have enough of an emotional connection left for a satisfactory marriage. In this situation you will probably feel exhausted and sad, rather than angry and resentful.

Alternatively, it's possible that you will both decide, openly or covertly, to continue with both the marriage and the affair. Some betraying partners choose this option, living a dual life, so as to hold on to family ties and to passion in their lives. Their spouses may be willing to go along with this arrangement because they fear being on their own or for economic reasons. Women who are older and financially dependent, who are depressed, or whose husbands are in the upper income brackets seem the most reluctant to end the marriage. If neither of you have done the work needed to resolve your issues, it may be that depression is limiting the energy you have available to make major changes, allowing the ménage à trois to continue.

If the Affair Resurfaces. The affair may resurface. Early in the healing process, if you are the betraying spouse, you may feel a lingering attachment to the affair partner. It exerts a strong pull and you may let yourself give in to it. It will be evident to your spouse, so admit the truth before you get back into the old pattern of lying. Hiding it may delay the day of judgment, but not for long. Your spouse is unlikely to ignore the warning signs this time.

If the two of you are working on your marriage, or anticipate doing so, you need to be honest. The lying is more deadly than the affair. If you've decided you don't want to work on your marriage, you still need to be honest. This means telling your spouse that the affair has resumed and that you've decided to leave the marriage. Becoming honest is part of the work you need to do to move ahead. Don't use the affair to silently convey the fact you are leaving—take responsibility for the decision you have made and give yourself a voice in telling your spouse of your decision.

Occasionally, there is deliberate contact between the betraying spouse and the third party, supposedly for purposes other than resuming the affair, such as answering a question about oneself. For example, Barbara wanted to know if Lew's love and concern for her had been real, so six months after ending the affair she met with Lew. If you're like Barbara, you will, at times, long to see your affair partner, but this will interfere with your own work. Barbara is again looking to her affair partner for external validation, rather than knowing that she has the capacity to feel passionate. Meeting with Lew without her husband's knowledge is risky. It's the secrecy that creates the risk. Barbara also put herself at risk of resuming the affair.

Danger Zones for Each of You. Danger zones exist for each of you following the revelation of an affair. Perhaps you're tempted to make a decision just to get things settled, not because you're ready to make a sound decision. You might consider adopting the rule that you won't make any decisions while you're in crisis. Give yourself plenty of time. Keep in mind that if you're no longer a thirty-something, your patterns have become more entrenched as you've gotten older, so change is slower for you than for a young adult. Offsetting that is the greater life experience you have. Don't make any decisions without understanding, both rationally and emotionally, where you are and where you are going.

At the opposite pole, but just as dangerous, is never making a decision, opting passively for months on end—or years—to stay with the status quo. You may be depressed. Sometimes depression sneaks up so gradually that you don't even realize you're depressed. If this is you, get professional help now to get yourself moving.

Because you're so competent at work and because you like to maintain control, you will be tempted to assume that you can do the work of healing and rebuilding by yourself. That is almost impossible. Your wounds go too deep, and your difficulty in paying attention to your emotions blocks you from the work you need to do. The cost of not getting help can mean continuing to cheat yourself rather than giving yourself a chance to heal.

Developing Realistic Expectations for Your Relationship. While you can heal your internal split between doing the right thing and paying attention to your own needs and feelings, you can't have it all. No one can, no matter who they're with. There are always choices to be made about how you spend your time and energy. In learning to use your emotions as well as your intellect, and by taking responsibility for your life, you become better equipped to make choices than in the past. Now you can make choices that are grounded in reality. You'll find that you're increasingly free of having to make the *right* choice—making a choice and dealing with it is sufficient.

What do you want in a partner *now*? Knowing that you can handle your pain, take responsibility for yourself, and otherwise manage your life, means that you no longer need the perfect partner to take care of you. You will be OK regardless. You will probably want another adult: someone who cares about you, someone who is emotionally present so that you can connect with each other, and someone who takes responsibility for himself or herself. You'll also want someone who pitches in with the task at hand, with whom you can negotiate, and who is willing to continue growing as the situation demands. You can expect to feel happy occasionally, satisfied at times, dissatisfied at other times, stressed on occasion, and a host of other feelings. If you're continuing to work on yourself and your relationship, you probably won't be bored.

Sexual Addiction Affairs

Sexual Addicts and their spouses have childhood wounds that go deeper than those of most others who have affairs. They extend back to childhood trauma and neglect that is extremely painful but that has been buried without being resolved. Physical and sexual abuse are commonly part of the picture, and shame is rampant. In a way Sexual Addicts have taken the road opposite that taken by the Split Selves. Where the Split Self tries to accommodate others in the hope of gaining approval, the Sexual Addict flees pain and tries to get others to provide care and comfort. The Sexual Addict is similar to the Split Self in that neither takes care of himself or herself.

Sexual Addiction takes many forms, but here we're going to focus on addiction to affairs. However, 83 percent of Sexual Addicts also have another addiction such as alcohol, drugs, or pornography.[1] Sexual addiction is particularly attractive because it taps into three areas of pleasure—arousal, satiation, and fantasy.[2] The Internet has added new possibilities for finding and pursuing sexual partners. For some sexual addicts the chat rooms and pornographic sites are sufficient, but for others, these sites are just a new arena in which to arrange sexual liaisons.

The public takes great interest in the affairs of Sexual Addicts, particularly those that hit the headlines. Sexual addiction has the capacity to fascinate and to horrify, maybe because it incorporates our most grandiose fantasies and our worst nightmares.

If you or your spouse is addicted to affairs, you're in pain and probably in danger as well, whether you've allowed yourself to feel it yet or not. You are both involved in a destructive dance, but because so many emotions are buried, you both deny just how bad things are. What you can't avoid, you rationalize.

When You Are the Sexual Addict

Your compulsive involvement in affairs is a way of hiding from the pain that lies in wait, a means of avoiding the emptiness buried inside. That is the function of all addictions, from alcohol to drugs to sex. As with other addictions, Sexual Addiction touches those around you. It is damaging to family relationships, to your children, and to your self-esteem. These days the risk is high of contracting AIDS or other sexually transmitted diseases, and possibly passing them on.

Motivations for Making Changes. Do you remember Ed, the Sexual Addict introduced in Chapter One? His shame about his behavior was so great that he covered up the truth, even from him-self, making it hard to think about getting help. It took a major crisis to bring the issue of Ed's sexual addiction out in the open. Ed's eighteen-year-old daughter, out on a date, bumped into her father propositioning a woman at a bar. She felt totally humiliated and told her father so the next day. Ed's shame was too great to fully suppress, and he started considering getting help to change his ways.

You, too, can put your shame to good use. Shame about your addictive behavior can provide a strong motivation for change. However, many Sexual Addicts don't pay attention to their shame, thus leaving themselves vulnerable to the decisions of others. For example, some addicts are fired for having sex with a subordinate, for using the company's expense account to pay for a sexual encounter, or for sexual harassment. Some are arrested for picking up prostitutes. Others are caught in compromising positions that are publicized. A few lose their marriage and their relationship with their children—but only a few because many spouses put up with the situation. Often it takes losses like these before the Sexual Addict sees the need for making changes.

The Sequence of Steps Toward Recovery. The crisis that shoves you into facing yourself presents you with a decision to make. Will you work toward stopping your addictive behavior, or not? Doing so will mean facing your personal demons, the pain and emptiness that have been chasing you for so long. It will also mean giving up your drug of choice, the activity that gives you some relief from your pain. Making a choice to stop your compulsive use of sex holds the promise, over the long haul, of giving you back your life.

You can't do this work alone. You need help: individual therapy, a group (possibly a twelve-step group), plus family therapy. If you decide to make changes in your behavior, get help right away. Call your local hotline or one of the organizations for sexual addicts to get names of therapists who are experienced in treating sexual addiction and for information about twelve-step groups (see Chapter Nine and the Resources section at the back of the book). Making the choice to get help is a major accomplishment.

In addition to the work outlined here for the Split Selves and in Chapter Six for Conflict Avoiders and Intimacy Avoiders, you will need to address the following issues:

- Typically Sexual Addicts have an addiction cycle in which they move from shame and promises to one's self "not to do that again" through bargaining to spotting the next conquest, to sex and satiation, and back to shame. Identify all the steps in your addiction cycle and the actions you can take to break out of your cycle at any point.
- You will need to learn how to feel again—not just shame or the thrill of the conquest, but the full range of your feelings. As you begin to crack through to your emotions, you will gain an understanding of the pain and trauma that impelled you to turn to sexual addiction. This is very difficult work.

- The skills of intimacy described in Chapter Six will be essential to your recovery. Expect that it will be especially difficult to learn how to take responsibility for yourself and to become honest with yourself and with others. Also read about nurturing the child inside you, earlier in this chapter.

- Work on rebuilding your relationships with your family.

- Ideally, all members of your family need to be involved in treatment so that each can untangle his or her own issues and so that you can work together on resolving the past and changing the present.

- Eventually, when you have your life on track, you will be ready to forgive yourself.

You can use *A Gentle Path Through the Twelve Steps,* a workbook by Patrick Carnes, as a guide in examining your behavior now, looking at how it developed, and exploring how you can change it.[3]

When You Are the Spouse of the Sexual Addict

As the spouse of a Sexual Addict, your part of the dance around Sexual Addiction is much like the dance of an alcoholic's spouse. You cover for your partner, you pick up the pieces, you give him good advice and try in every way you can think of to change his behavior. Ed's wife, Michelle (from Chapter One), kept thinking, "If I do just a little bit more, then he'll appreciate me and be willing to make some changes." When she does this, Michelle is taking responsibility for Ed's behavior, behavior over which she has absolutely no control. However, as long as she focuses on Ed's behavior she doesn't have to feel the pain and despair stemming from the wounds she suffered as a child. Taking responsibility for changing Ed also makes her feel needed—even though Ed is unappreciative.

Steps Toward Recovery. You too need to engage in your own recovery. Much of the work outlined for the Split Self Spouse and in Chapter Six for the Conflict Avoiders and Intimacy Avoiders is also yours to do.

In particular, you need to learn to pay attention to what you are feeling and to give yourself a voice. Your voice has been missing for a long time—maybe all your life. It has been missing because as a child you felt it was too dangerous to speak up. As an adult it is possible to learn how to speak up about uncomfortable or dangerous situations.

Taking responsibility only for yourself and not for your spouse will be key in changing the dynamic between the two of you. Doing so will not make your spouse change, but will start you moving along a different path. That path is one that leads you toward taking care of yourself, something that is totally foreign to you. It is a difficult path, one that requires you to pay attention to what you are feeling rather than to rely on your old habit of busying yourself with changing your spouse's behavior.

Getting the Help You Need. Just as your spouse needs help to accomplish the changes that are necessary, so do you. You're used to doing everything by yourself, but the addictive dance is too big for that. You might start by reading *Co-Dependent No More* by Melody Beattie for an overview of the issues facing the spouse of an addict.[4]

Get into individual therapy with a therapist who is familiar with sexual addiction and with co-dependency (see Chapter Nine). In addition to the other issues you need to address in therapy, it's likely that you have some issues around your own sexuality that you will want to explore.

Find out if twelve-step groups for the spouses of sexual addicts meet in your area (numbers to call and e-mail addresses are listed in the Resources section at the end of this book). If so, get yourself there. If not, get yourself to a group for spouses of any sort of addiction.

Marital therapy may be useful at a later date if both of you resolve some of your individual issues and are ready to work on the marriage. Family therapy can also help each family member untangle issues that were generated in response to the Sexual Addiction.

The Road Ahead

The two of you may have a chance of working out a decent marriage if you each get help and tackle your own issues, and in addition, work on your relationship issues with each other. Or it may be that so much damage has been done that getting help can lead to a decision to end the marriage. If only the betrayed spouse gets help, it's probable that the marriage will end. In a great many cases, no one gets help and the addictive behavior continues for as long as life allows.

Sexual Addiction is only touched upon here, but you know that the wounds are deep and painful, and that the work required is difficult. Give yourself the time, the space, and the commitment to heal.

Summary

Healing early wounds is possible for Split Selves and for Sexual Addicts. Give yourself the gift of getting help so that your wounds are no longer what drive you. With help, you can learn how to put your life on a different and positive course, one that honors your deepest emotions and frees you to be yourself with others.

Chapter Eight

Rebuilding When Your Marriage Ends with an Affair

Ending your marriage well leads to a
good beginning.

Colleen left Oliver to be with Adam. Oliver finds it tempting to put all the blame for ending the marriage on Colleen's affair. That way, it's not anything he did that made Colleen leave. Besides, Oliver doesn't totally want to slam the door on Colleen. She might change her mind yet about coming back. Colleen too wants to see the affair as the reason she left Oliver. She doesn't want to think of herself as abandoning her marriage; she's just fallen in love with Adam. However, before Adam appeared on the scene, her decision to leave was already in the works because of problems, some buried, some not, that she and Oliver were experiencing.

Colleen's affair is a typical Exit Affair. She unconsciously chose an affair as her escape route so she wouldn't have to go through the incredibly difficult experience of speaking the truth about wanting to leave. But now she's stuck with even more pain, and both she and Oliver want to run ever faster from it. The affair is now the focus. Colleen is running toward the affair, and Oliver's head is spinning around with visions and speculations about her affair.

The affair is not the main course here; the decision to end the marriage is. The purpose of the affair is to avoid taking responsibility for ending the marriage. Exiters are people who can't say no without giving reasons and justifications, who are so afraid of offending or provoking conflict that they procrastinate, eventually acting out what they're afraid to say in words, and thereby creating even greater conflict. They have difficulty with endings of all sorts. Exiters are Conflict Avoiders at heart, but this is not a Conflict Avoidance Affair. Those affairs are designed to get the partner's attention so as to start repairing the marriage. The function of the Exit Affair is to end the marriage. The affair, characterized as "true love," provides an acceptable reason for leaving. The affair lets the betrayed partner off the hook too—it's nothing they've done; it's that sneaky, lying third party that broke up the marriage. Sometimes couple friends help each other end both marriages through an affair.

When your marriage ends with an affair, you and your spouse have a lot of unfinished business with each other. You may not have talked with each other about the all-important fact that the marriage is ending and why. The affair has been a barricade blocking the hard issues, but the issues are still there. They show up in the betraying spouse's impatience to get it over with and in the betrayed spouse's obsession. It's easy for a dance of pain and retaliation to get going and for common sense to be set aside.

It doesn't have to be that way. Whether you're the one leaving the marriage or the one who's been left, it is possible to come through this experience with integrity and be the better for it. The good news is that you *can* achieve closure. The bad news is you won't achieve closure with each other for several years. Your work in the meantime is to end your marriage with dignity, get your own life in order, and learn the skills of intimacy. It will require everything you've got.

When You're the One Ending the Marriage

Ending your marriage with an affair seems easier than trying to convince your spouse that the marriage should end. An affair justifies calling it quits—it makes clear that there are problems; it's not just your imagination or your impatience. The problem is that the sequence of things is backwards: you haven't talked straight to your partner about your decision to end your marriage. Maybe you fear your partner's wrath, your guilt has you tongue-tied, you don't know how to persuade your spouse that it's the right decision, you're afraid of being lonely, or you prefer that your partner do the ending. Perhaps you've never seen a relationship end well so you are laying low and sliding away trying to prevent the "War of the Roses." Perhaps the third party will serve as a shield, catching the flak in the war zone between you and your spouse. Or does the affair push away the ghosts of past losses? What makes it easier for *you* to use an affair to end the marriage rather than tell your spouse that you are leaving? Whatever your answer, make a note of it—that issue is a piece of your unfinished business.

Ending a marriage is never easy, but ending your marriage with an affair is one of the most traumatic ways to do it. You still have to grieve for your losses, even if the only thing left was your dreams. Now you have guilt and shame to resolve as well. These feelings come from the lies and the secrecy, and the knowledge of the pain your affair has caused.

It doesn't seem like it at first. The affair feels so good after all the difficulties in the marriage that it crystallizes the semi-decision you've made to leave. The affair is your permission slip that says you've got a good enough reason to be dismissed early. In our society, love seems like the perfect reason. But love can be cruel.

"I didn't know how to tell Nancy that I was leaving her," said Bryan. "I just couldn't do that to her. But I felt like such a wimp! Here I was with this woman I've known for thirteen years, and I couldn't face her with what I was doing! I felt like such a little kid. Of course I covered it up from myself for a long time. I leaned on my lover to make me feel better, and she did in many ways, but I still felt crummy. It was only after she and I split up that I had to face how bad I felt inside and how ashamed I was, especially with my kids. I got real depressed for a while. Finally I got some help and started coming to terms with myself. I'm not sorry I left Nancy—our marriage was pretty well gone, but I'm sorry about how I did it. I know she went through a lot of extra pain and so did the kids."

Power and powerlessness had been issues for Bryan and Nancy in their marriage. Bryan's way of leaving illustrated just how powerless he felt. Nancy felt equally powerless when Bryan abandoned her for another woman. Each has had to work on finding new ways of handling feelings of powerlessness and on giving themselves a voice.

Just before separation, the affair crisis comes to a head. In a final dash to avoid pain, some destructive behaviors can take over. For example, Mike stopped returning his kids' phone calls, stopped taking his medication for high blood pressure, came home at any hour or not at all, purchased expensive gifts for his lover that dented the family budget, took time from work to be with Sharon, and put off every household task that wasn't an immediate crisis. It was as if he couldn't get enough of Sharon—and he couldn't do enough to avoid his wife, Sue. Any time Sue complained, he turned it around so that she became the problem. It was because she gained weight, because she didn't care about what he felt, because she was just too demanding.

For a while, Sue begged and cajoled, trying to convince Mike that she loved him, and that she would do whatever he needed her to do to prove it. Of course nothing she did convinced Mike, because his decision to leave had long since been made. Much of his provocative behavior was unconsciously designed to get Sue to end the marriage. He didn't want to be the bad guy. If Sue kicked him out, she would share the responsibility for ending the marriage. Finally, Mike realized that Sue was not going to do it for him, and he took steps to start the process of separating.

When You've Been Left

Your husband has just told you he's leaving—to move in with another woman. If you are being left through an affair you probably feel devastated and furious, but you wouldn't feel much better without the affair. You focus on the affair—it gives you someone to blame and a place to put all those feelings that are overwhelming you. The affair feels like an alien from outer space. What does it have to do with *your* marriage? You're red hot one minute and ice cold the next. You question the very beliefs you've held dear—beliefs about yourself, your partner, your marriage, even the predictability of life.

The affair raises doubts about your sense of reality—what is reality? If this is reality, why didn't you see it? Maybe some retaliatory action is needed to push things back in place. If that doesn't work, at least you'll have a bit of a defense. When all else fails, you get off on fantasies of making your spouse pay or ensuring that "justice" is done. Be careful here. Retaliation usually comes back to haunt *you*.

Creative Substitutes for Blame and Retaliation

The theme underlying your obsession is "I'm innocent and you're totally to blame" (for everything, ever!). Blame and retaliation are part of the obsessive process that lets you avoid your pain and anger. They're unworthy substitutes—they're not empowering and they keep you in a victim stance. Instead of getting even, get angry—do something safe but symbolic to unload. The only ground rules are no damage to people (including yourself) or property, and no mess to clean up. For example, you can write a letter to your spouse detailing all the horrible things you want to say. Don't send it (ever), but file it away in a safe place to read later. You can stick pins in a doll you name for your spouse. You might write down all the words you can think of that describe your spouse. Or throw ice cubes at a cement block wall as you imagine your spouse standing there. You can probably come up with other creative ways to unload. These ways to unload will give you some temporary relief from your rage, but only if you let yourself *feel* your pain and anger as you engage in them. If you stay in your head, they won't help. Remember that anger is a normal and essential part of the grief process.

Jim agonized every morning as he came to consciousness about "what he had done wrong." And every night between fitful bouts of sleep he ruminated about what he could do to get Kate back, and what he could do to get even. Kate had left him for another man. "How dare she! How could she do this to me?! I'll make her pay! But wait a minute—maybe she regrets her mistake. Maybe she'll come crawling back. No, she won't crawl. But it's obvious I'm right. After all, I'd never have an affair. That guy took advantage of her. I feel like beating him up. Sure, Kate and I had our problems, but we can get that worked out. We'll do that marriage counseling she always wanted to do—but she'll have to prove she deserves another chance. But that's a stupid idea—go through more of this?!"

It turned out that nothing Jim did worked. Kate was gone for good—not just gone but living with another man. Jim gave up his dreams of getting Kate back and focused instead on his anger and his fantasies of revenge for being so humiliated and so hurt. Secret thoughts of strangling the other man or running over Kate helped Jim defend against his pain at being abandoned. But they didn't make him feel better.

Exit Affairs like Kate's leave a lot of litter behind for the abandoned spouse to deal with alone. Any affair that leads to divorce is painful, but the cold abandonment of the Exit Affair accentuates feelings of powerlessness and humiliation for the abandoned spouse. It's bad enough to be discarded on your own merits, but to be replaced by someone else and then be lied to is enraging and humiliating. Meanwhile your spouse appears to be living the good life, turning to the affair partner for good words, a soothing touch, and refuge from you, while avoiding pain and responsibility.

If the affair is your partner's excuse to end the marriage, there is little you can do to change that decision, but you don't have to take responsibility for doing the painful emotional work that your partner is avoiding: the work of deciding to end the marriage. You have enough pain of your own so let your spouse take responsibility for choosing to end the marriage.

The work facing Kate and Jim is much the same as for couples rebuilding their marriage after an affair. The big difference is that

Kate and Jim will be working separately on rebuilding their individual lives, and doing so just when they are faced with the emotional loss and the stresses of divorce. It's a double whammy—especially for Jim, who doesn't have a partner to soothe his pain. Each will need to work their way through the emotional steps of divorce, in addition to finishing off the unfinished business they brought to the marriage. Learning the skills of intimacy described in Chapter Six is part of this process.

Moving from Obsession to Reevaluation

Obsession usually lasts longer with an Exit Affair than with other types of affairs. The revenge and retaliation are part of a power struggle to validate who's right and who's wrong. If you're declared the winner, what do you really have? Everybody needs validation, particularly when the bottom falls out, but it's shaky to base your worth on making your ex the bad guy. The validation that really works has to come from inside you, and it's not validation about the affair but about you as a person.

It's very tempting to blame the third party so as to avoid facing the fact that your spouse wasn't really coerced by the third party but chose to leave. Blaming the third party also keeps you from having to examine your own contribution to the end of the marriage. At the very least, you can explore why you picked this partner, and why you stayed for as long as you did. You need to move from a victim stance to one of owning your own share of the marital problems. To make this shift, you need to give your pain and anger (not resentment, blame, or self-pity) a voice.

During the obsessive period, you will both reevaluate each other and reinterpret the meaning of your marriage. You may try to validate yourself by believing that your partner is and was a terrible person and that everything about the marriage was a fraud. This perspective comes from an all-or-nothing, right-versus-wrong framework—if your spouse is wrong, then you are right. This kind of thinking is also an attempt to master the facts so that you can understand rationally what is going on and regain control of your life. However, nothing about marriage or divorce is this simple.

Voicing Your Feelings

The more you pay attention to your emotions and give them a voice, the more quickly you will move beyond obsession. The person you need to voice your feelings to is the partner who betrayed you. You may want to do this in person, on the phone, in a counseling session, or in writing. Choose your timing and your words carefully. This is not an attack session. Your partner may or may not listen to you. The important element here is not whether your partner listens or accepts what you are saying, but your ability to take a stand and validate yourself instead of stewing in silent resentment. You are, in effect, saying, "I feel hurt, and I'm angry at you for all the pain you've caused me. I'm sick and tired of feeling hurt and I'm not going to listen to any more criticism of what I've done." Only say it when you believe it. When you have had your say, you are more able to hear others, including your children.

As you give up obsessing about the affair and get on with your own life, you can begin to see why you picked your spouse, what your blind spots are, and where you contributed to the breakdown of your marriage. It's at this point that you can begin to reclaim those things that were good about your spouse and your marriage. This sequential reinterpretation of your marriage enables you to put important pieces in place. It is after this work has been done that you are ready to forgive each other. This may be several years after you separate.

The Emotional Steps of Divorce

The emotional process of divorce is a long one—without an affair it's a couple of years after you separate at best. With an affair it takes longer for each of you. For the betraying spouse, the affair softens the pain of loss and delays examining the real issues that led to divorce.

For the betrayed spouse the affair is an additional wound and the obsession about the affair delays getting to the real work of separating emotionally. You and your ex will be out of synch with each other much of the time, beginning a couple of years before you separate, as one or the other of you begins to consider ending the marriage.

It's very tempting to play out the issues around power, blame, and pain in the divorce courts. It's like a tennis game with only a win-lose ending permitted. One spouse serves with the affair, the other volleys back by hiring an attorney, and you are off and running. You each have stand-ins to take the heat instead of facing the real issues yourselves and learning from them as you end your marriage. You have better options available.

Take plenty of time to move through these steps as you end your marriage:

Steps for the Betraying Spouse

- If you've decided to end the marriage, don't wait for your spouse to do it for you. Continuing to lie and to hide, telling your partner nothing or saying "everything's OK" while you disappear overnight, is crazymaking. Tempers flare and abuse can occur in a flash in this situation. Take responsibility for your decision to end the marriage.

- Tell your partner of your decision to end the marriage (or to separate) in a gentle but firm way. Refrain from attacking or bad-mouthing your spouse or making comparisons with the third party. If your spouse asks, "Is there someone else?" tell the truth. If your spouse didn't have a pretty good idea of the situation, this question wouldn't come up. Have this discussion in private, not in front of the kids. If you can't do it alone, go with your spouse to see a counselor who can help you talk about your decision.

- After you talk with your spouse, plan together how to tell your children that you are separating (see Chapter Ten) and do so.

- Consider living apart from your affair partner for a period of time after you separate. Living together immediately with your affair partner lets you avoid the work you need to do in sorting out yourself, your marriage, and if you have children, your new way of being a parent. Go ahead and see your affair partner but give yourself separate space to assess and work on your own issues.

- Your involvement with your affair partner won't provide you with an emotional divorce. No relationship can make up for your losses or emotional wounds, or make you feel whole. Your emotional divorce is going to be up to you, and it will be harder than you think.

- Negotiate with your ex the children's time and their contact with the third party. Remember that kids need time to grieve for their family as they've known it before they have to deal with parents' new relationships. Children are deeply unsettled when a new partner is on the scene immediately after their parents separate. They do not do well with this, so keep your time with your children separate from time with your affair partner for at least the first six months. See Chapter Ten for additional guidance on helping your children.

Steps for the Betrayed Spouse

- Don't spy or check up on your spouse. It may bother your spouse but it will drive *you* nuts!

- You're not going to trust your spouse right now, except possibly in limited areas. For example, you might trust your spouse as a parent, based on past performance. Even there you'll probably feel like reassessing whether this trust is warranted. If it is, grant that much trust. The more areas that can remain uncontaminated the better for all of you.

- Recognize that the legal process of divorce won't help you feel better about your partner's affair. The mythology that you will have your day in court is just that: mythology. These days it's a rare court that cares about adultery or uses it as the basis for making decisions (although your attorney may attempt to inflame matters with charges of adultery). It's almost always better to keep information about the affair out of the legal proceedings. Make your decisions on a practical basis, not an emotional one. Be aware that *the legal system doesn't provide an emotional divorce, only a legal divorce.*

- If you're tempted to engage in a legal battle, learn how the legal system in your area actually works. Legal battles usually have one or more of the following purposes: to prove that you, the betrayed spouse, are the better person and didn't deserve to be abandoned; to prove that you, the betraying spouse, are justified in leaving; to prevent any additional losses; and to get even with your ex. The legal system isn't very good at the first three. It is best at getting even, but the price will be paid by both of you and by your children.

- Custody tends to be a hot issue. You may want custody because you fear being alone, or as compensation for losing your spouse, or to punish your spouse. Consider the legacy you want to leave your kids. In ten or twenty years, will they view your efforts as protective of them or will they remember the pain of the custody battle or the loss of the other parent? Custody fights are extremely costly, both emotionally and financially. Save your money and your kids by focusing on what your kids need.

- Once you've moved beyond grieving, keep your eye on where you are now and the direction you're going rather than where you've been.

Steps for Both of You

- Don't bad-mouth your ex. It makes you look bad, and it feels bad, especially to your children. You've got more important things to do.

- Resist using the legal system's opportunities for power struggles and custody fights. Usually these fights are a very expensive and ineffective substitute for grieving. If you're in such a fight, it's likely that one or both of you are stuck in the angry part of the grief process in an attempt to ward off your pain. The end result is increased pain and empty pockets.

- Think about using mediation to make your decisions about parenting, financial support, and property. It's much more user friendly than the adversarial process, and the two of you maintain control of your decisions. It may seem strange to consider working together on separating when you want to wring each other's necks, but it will pay off in reduced conflict and bitterness, decisions tailored to fit your particular situation, and the groundwork laid for cooperative parenting. Mediation doesn't require that you like each other—it assumes there's conflict and helps you manage it while you are settling your financial matters and deciding on parenting arrangements for your children (see Chapter Nine).

- Let yourself grieve. Your marriage was important, as were your hopes and dreams for it, and you have to grieve before you can let go and move on. Grieving has several steps: shock and disbelief, anger, pain, sadness, and finally letting go. There's an old saying in alcohol recovery, that "You can't heal what you can't feel." Let yourself *feel* each emotion, without trying to suppress or dismiss it. Remember that feelings are different from actions: you feel however you feel, but you have choices about your behavior. Feelings run their course when you give them their due, so don't worry. You are not going to feel like this forever.

- One of the biggest mistakes either of you can make is to remarry before you are emotionally divorced. Give yourself all the time you need. Delay making any decision about remarriage until you have finished the work of your first marriage. Expect the entire process to take you at least three years after you separate.

- Keep in mind that forgiveness will be possible at some future time. It can't be rushed, and doesn't need to be. Read Chapter Twelve for ideas about when and how this might occur.

Danger Zones

The danger zone for Exiters, as for others involved in affairs, is when you shut down emotionally. You probably already know the situations where you tend to get scared and shut down. Your job is to keep feeling, especially when it's painful or scary, so that you can keep moving. Following are typical ways of shutting down when your marriage ends with an affair.

Depression

You're more at risk for depression if you're the spouse who's been left, rather than the one who did the leaving. When you're depressed you're down, you've got no energy, nothing holds any interest. You don't sleep or you sleep too much. You lose interest in eating or you overeat. Depression can get so painful that you even think seriously of suicide. Here, you are putting your anger into a U-turn and directing it at yourself.

Gina felt powerless after her husband left her. Her anger came to the fore as a defense against her powerlessness. However, she turned her anger on herself, rationalizing that she wasn't really angry at anyone else; her husband wasn't a bad person, and she didn't want to be "one of those divorced women who are always angry." The reality is that her husband left her for another woman, saying he didn't want to work on the marriage. Gina is a "nice" person, to a fault, and it's tearing her apart. The only way out for Gina was to feel her feelings—powerlessness, anger, and all—without turning them on herself.

Some depression is normal after splitting up, as part of the grieving process. However, if you're unable to function or your depression is too painful, or it goes on and on, get professional help to get you moving again. *If you feel like hurting yourself get help immediately.*

Blaming

Presenting yourself as a victim and blaming others, especially your ex and the third party, won't make you feel better—but it's a way to feel less vulnerable when you're the betrayed spouse. As a victim, your energy goes into soliciting sympathy without taking responsibility. You settle for blaming others rather than expressing your own emotions. Your message is, "Somebody did me wrong, so you owe me." Victims are angry people and it comes through. Your friends will only listen to this story for so long.

Betraying spouses also fall into the victim trap, blaming the ex so as to justify the affair, and not taking responsibility for the decision to end the marriage or for any of the problems in the marriage.

Hiding Behind Your Children

"You left us!" yells Anna to her estranged husband, Al, who has left Anna for another woman. Her statement sounds as if the children are equal partners with Anna in the marriage. It's important to remember that children are children, not marital partners. Or Anna's statement could be construed as implying that it's OK for Al to leave her but it's not OK for him to leave the children. This kind of comment is a way of using your children to make your spouse feel guilty. For your kids' sake, leave them out of it. Let yourself feel the tremendous pain that your spouse has left *you*. Speak about your hurt as a spouse rather than as the children's parent.

Betraying spouses are also tempted to hide behind the children. Comments such as "The kids really like her" are meant to justify the affair, but the reality is that they rub salt into the betrayed spouse's wounds. Instead, consider and discuss what your children really need right now. See Chapter Ten for suggestions.

Don't turn to your children for comfort, especially now. They need both of you to be their parents and to comfort them. Read Chapter Nine for ideas about who you can turn to for comfort and confide in safely.

Waiting for Your Spouse to Come Back

If you're the betrayed spouse it's likely that you've cast your ex in the role of rescuer, probably because your former spouse has rescued you, or promised to, before. Waiting pathetically does not make you feel good nor does it make you attractive to your spouse. You've got a slim chance of making your spouse feel guilty enough to come back—but if your spouse comes back on that basis, what do you really have? Not someone who wants to be with you because of love and affection for *you*. Start taking responsibility for your own life by doing small things that get you moving. You count too.

For example, one woman decided to move her husband's favorite chair out of the living room so it wasn't a constant reminder. Then she hired a neighborhood teen to fix the flapping screen door that her husband never got around to. As she got momentum, she realized she didn't need her husband to come back for her to have a life. She stated, "I don't want to be with someone whose party is elsewhere."

Waiting to Be Rescued

Although both spouses are susceptible to waiting for a rescuer, this is true more often for the betrayed spouse. The betraying spouse may be at risk if the affair ends. When you don't rebuild your own life it means you're waiting for someone else to come along and swoop you up, or you simply don't want to have to be responsible for yourself. It's a decision to give up on yourself, though usually an unconscious one. You act as if your life is over. Depression is usually part of this picture.

Continuing Rage

Out-and-out rage, generally on the part of the betrayed spouse, is a defense against immense feelings of powerlessness when you've been pushed beyond your limit. The affair has opened up some old wounds. Get professional help before you do something you regret.

The Party Scene

Living a very social life is another way to hide out from yourself. It's fun, it's distracting, and maybe you'll meet the perfect person this time. However, it keeps you from healing and growing. This is a danger zone for each of you.

Quick Remarriage

Marrying on the rebound is a way of trying to skip steps in the emotional process of divorce. Even when you're the one who wants out, you need to go through a grieving process and a period of getting to know yourself.

All these paths to emotional quicksand are about avoiding being responsible for yourself and your feelings. When you recognize that you're stuck, stop, take a deep breath, and look inside to see what's got you scared. Then take the steps described in Chapter Six to regain responsibility for yourself.

When the Affair Becomes the Marriage

You start out at a disadvantage if you marry your affair partner too soon. That doesn't mean you can't make it work—it just means you've got extra baggage from the affair that can poison your wedded bliss.

A quick remarriage to the third party is dangerous, no matter how wonderful the person seems. You haven't taken the time to grieve, to come to terms with your individual issues, or learn what went wrong in your first marriage. Until you've made major changes in how you relate to a partner, you are going to pick the same kind of person again—someone who represents your unfinished business from childhood. If you're the same, your new partner will also be the same, even if the outside of the package looks different. Living alone for at least a year (preferably longer) is an essential part of closing the book on your marriage.

Honesty is an issue when you begin your marriage with your affair partner. You're connected through your affair, which has tentacles of shame and distrust. If you lied to your former spouse, it means you have the capacity to lie. Will you do the same in this marriage? Do you have the willingness to be honest in the face of discomfort? To be totally honest—about everything? This is an important issue for the two of you to discuss openly. What is different now?

Some couples do well as long as they are united against a third person. Joining forces against your former spouses as you ended your marriages can be emotionally intense. Now you will need to start exploring what you have in common besides the sexual attraction and wanting to end your prior marriages. Are you headed in the same direction? For example, do you both want children? Do you expect your spouse to be a nest-builder or an adventurous companion? How do the two of you plan to handle big decisions? These aspects of your relationship won't be apparent until you have moved beyond the crisis phase of ending your marriage and embarked on rebuilding your life.

Look into the future as you consider marrying. A big age gap between the two of you suggests that problems may arise a decade or so from now. Younger women who team up with older men at the peak of their power face a different situation in fifteen or so years. Their husbands will be embarking on old age, with declining abilities, just at the time the wives are hitting their stride. If this happens in your future, will you still find your husband attractive and want to care for him? Or when your husband can't keep up with you, will you be drawn to a more powerful man your own age? Will you decide to divorce your husband then, or will you solve your dilemma with an affair, or in some other way? This is a difficult issue that the two of you need to discuss together before you marry.

If you decide to marry, the skills of intimacy described in Chapter Six will be important in making this marriage work. These skills are paying attention to your feelings, being honest, owning responsibility for yourself, giving yourself a voice, and allowing yourself to be emotionally vulnerable with your partner. By using these skills you give your marriage a better chance for success.

If either of you has children, making room for them in your family is essential. That means putting time and energy into getting to know your spouse's children, and working cooperatively on decision making and matters of discipline. The children will probably be moving between mom's house and dad's house, and that requires cooperation between the households. Let yourself see your spouse's children as children, not as intruders in your marriage or as emissaries of your former rival. If you can love them as well, all the better.

Once you and your affair partner live together on a daily basis, your dreams of the knight on the white horse or of the fairy godmother crash into reality. You've got decisions to make about where you're going to live, discipline issues with the kids, refrigerators that give up the ghost, and all the other annoyances of real life. You're impatient, irritated, exhausted, and disappointed—not the stuff that dreams are made of. Can you let go of the fantasy and deal effectively with all the vicissitudes of real life?

Will you make time for each other—time to talk, time for fun, and time for intimacy? It's in this personal time that you can be most yourself with each other. It's in the vulnerability of being known for who you are that true intimacy thrives, and the intimacy helps you get through the difficult times in your marriage and your life.

Summary

When your marriage ends with an affair you have a long and difficult road to travel. You can use it to learn better ways to live your life, whether you're alone or in a new relationship. Take the time you need, but keep yourself moving along the road.

Chapter Nine

Getting Help That Is Helpful

Defining what you want and making sound choices
are important tools for your journey.

Affairs are so painful and so confusing that many people choose to
get professional help to untangle the situation. Numerous resources
are available, but they vary in approach, in experience, and in competence. Knowing what you're looking for and what questions to
ask will make a difference in who you select and in your overall sat-
isfaction. In other words, educated consumers have the best chance
of getting the best services.

Since affairs trigger such strong feelings in so many people, it is
very important to be selective when choosing a professional. It also
pays to be selective about advice from friends and relatives who
want to help. Friends have some wonderful resources and some
not-so-wonderful ones. Find out why your friend thinks a particular resource is a good one for you. Skip the resources who focus on
punishment and revenge. Instead, look for resources who will help
you be your best.

Therapists

With an affair, chances are you can benefit by seeing a counselor or
therapist (these terms are interchangeable). If you feel depressed or
as if you're coming apart, if you're stuck in the obsessive phase, if
you're so angry you're a danger to yourself or others, if you can't
decide what to do about your marriage, or if you don't know what

you feel, a therapist can help. In choosing a therapist it is essential to find someone with expertise in treating affairs.

Finding a Good Therapist

Questions you can ask a prospective therapist include:

- *What is the therapist's philosophy about keeping secrets in couples work?*
  Don't see a therapist who will keep secrets. A good therapist won't reveal your secrets for you, but will help you come clean with your partner. A relationship built on falsehoods is doomed, and secrets are falsehoods.

- *What values or moral stance about affairs does the therapist have?*
  An appropriate stance is to approach affairs in terms of the pain, the underlying issues, the need to develop new relationship skills, and using the affair as an opportunity to make significant changes. Blame and taking sides have no place here. Getting a therapist to beat up on your betraying spouse won't help either—and a good therapist won't take this approach.
  The therapist can not make the betraying spouse end the affair. A therapist who insists that the affair end may just drive it underground. When the affair is continuing, it's more useful to keep it out in the open. However, the therapist will probably recommend individual work, possibly with an occasional couples session, until the affair has ended and there is a mutual commitment to work on the marriage.

- *What training and experience does the therapist have in working with couples and with affairs?*
  Many good couples therapists don't have training specifically in working with affairs. Unfortunately, such training is usually not part of the graduate curriculum. However, many experienced therapists do good work with affairs, having

learned through trial and error. Training available on this subject is generally in the form of continuing education workshops.

- *Does the therapist see his or her role as saving the marriage?*
  The therapist's role is to help the two of you clarify your situation; not to make your decisions for you about whether or not to end the marriage. A competent therapist will help you examine your emotions and your options concerning divorce, and may suggest that you slow down enough to do so, but will leave the decisions to you. Remember that it is not possible nor is it the therapist's responsibility to make an unwilling spouse stay in the marriage.
  Avoid a therapist who makes comments like "We don't discuss divorce here" *or* "You really need to end your marriage." Either approach cuts off your exploration of your situation and limits your options.

Asking About Credentials

You probably wonder what kind of therapist you should see. The mental health field includes many disciplines. Those most likely to be familiar with couples work and with affairs are marriage and family therapists, clinical social workers, clinical psychologists, and mental health counselors. Make sure that your therapist is licensed by the state. If your state does not have licensing for that discipline, ask about the professional organizations the person belongs to and the level of membership (professional, associate, or general). Find out how many years the person has been in practice. You don't want a beginner when you're struggling with an affair.

Your initial sessions will be either individual or couples therapy, or a combination of both. Whether or not you decide on couples therapy, your therapist should be skilled in working with couples as well as with individuals.

Description of a Good Counselor or Therapist

- Pays attention to your feelings and helps you to do the same.
- Is empathic.
- Insists on an honest process, including not keeping the affair a secret.
- Helps you understand the unfinished business that underlies your problem areas.
- Helps you learn how to change your behavior.
- Won't make decisions for you but encourages you to make your own.
- Spurs you to break old habits and explore new directions.
- Takes an active approach in helping you get beyond ruminating about the affair.
- Calls you on it when you play victim or cop out on yourself.
- Is nonjudgmental.

When you don't want to use the therapists suggested by your friends, other options exist for finding someone good. Many employers offer Employee Assistance Programs (EAPs) that include brief counseling and referral services. EAPs usually offer good referrals to therapists and also to other resources. Professional organizations such as the local Society for Clinical Social Work and the Marriage and Family Therapy Association also make referrals. Hotlines are another source for referrals, although their referrals are usually limited to public and nonprofit organizations.

If you choose to use your health insurance, you are likely to encounter many restrictions stemming from managed care's concern about dollars. You are sure to be limited in the number of sessions approved and in the amount that insurance will pay toward each session. To use your insurance, your therapist will be required to reveal personal information about you.

Nonprofessionals may override the judgment of your therapist about the treatment you need. Many of the more experienced therapists are not approved providers with managed care plans because they oppose the loss of client confidentiality and the role of insurance companies in determining treatment. However, some coverage may be provided for these therapists if your plan has an out-of-network option.

Once you begin therapy, your responsibilities are to pay attention to your emotions and talk about what you are feeling, to examine your behavior and work on changing detrimental patterns, and to stick with the process when it feels uncomfortable. That's usually when you are getting close to some old and painful issues. It's often when therapy is the most productive.

If your children are showing signs of stress, they may benefit by seeing a therapist too. Common ways that children show stress are by misbehaving, being too good, or becoming depressed. Talk with each child's teacher to find out more about how the child is coping in school, and to discuss whether your child might benefit by talking to the school counselor. Get help from your own therapist in how to talk to your children about what is happening in your family. Ask whether a family session might be useful, and raise any questions you have about therapy for your children. Keep in mind that children benefit greatly when parents are actively working on their own issues.

Religious Institutions and Spiritual Leaders

The role of religious institutions and spiritual leaders varies from one extreme to another when it comes to affairs. Even within a single denomination, the differences are great. A few churches and synagogues do truly minister to members who have gotten involved in an affair. For example, a church in Atlanta, Georgia, uses a group of leaders to help the members deal with an affair, which is framed as a family conflict. In many other churches and synagogues, ministers regularly counsel parishioners about marital problems, including affairs. Others, however, limit themselves to preaching about the sin of adultery. Occasionally the media report that someone in the latter group has been doing some personal testing of the subject.

If you're religious and you believe it would be helpful to talk to your minister, rabbi, or priest, by all means do so. Some have training as counselors and can be very helpful. Others offer compassion and a supportive spiritual approach. To ensure you don't get hellfire and damnation when you're looking for compassion, ask about the approach used in your church or synagogue. Talking to your spiritual leader does not replace seeing a counselor, unless the person is trained as a mental health professional and has time to offer counseling on a regular basis.

Mediation

If your marriage is ending, consider mediation as a desirable alternative to the traditional win-lose adversarial process of divorce. Mediation is a kinder (and cheaper) process for deciding on your parenting arrangements, your property, and your finances. Mediation is based on the idea that by working together you can tailor decisions that best suit the two of you and your children. Mediators do not make your decisions for you, and they do not take sides. Rather, they are trained to guide separating and divorcing couples through a problem-solving process of identifying goals, evaluating options, and coming to agreement on financial, parenting, and property issues. You both will need to make full disclosure of your financial situation and provide documentation. At the end of mediation, you will each need an attorney. Attorneys can only represent one person. Thus one attorney prepares the legal paperwork and advises one spouse, and the other attorney reviews the paperwork and advises the other spouse. Couples who mediate successfully don't need to engage in an adversarial legal process or court battles.

As noted in Chapter Eight, you don't have to like each other to mediate. It's normal to be hurt and angry when an affair is part of the picture. Everyone who is divorcing has issues around trust. You can still turn to mediation. Mediation helps because everything is put on the table and talked through. In a few situations, mediation is not a good choice, as when one spouse is hiding or transferring assets, taking drugs, or seriously mentally ill.

Your children will need a great deal from each of you. Mediation helps you decide how to make sure your children get what they need. You will also become more knowledgeable about the details of your finances, and therefore better equipped to negotiate. Mediation is the adult version of helping kids resolve a fight over a toy they both love.

Very few states have licensing or certification for mediators, and state requirements tend to be minimal. The Academy of Family Mediators (617-674-2663, or www.igc.org/afm) is the recognized professional organization for family and divorce mediators and has promoted high standards for mediators. The Academy can provide you with referrals to mediators in your area. Ask for a mediator who has met the Academy's standards for the Practitioner level of membership. In addition, some state courts provide mediation services. Usually these are offered only to couples who are locked in to a custody contest.

In checking out a mediator's qualifications, find out:

- How long has the mediator been practicing mediation? (Many mediators have been "in practice" for some time, but in another profession.)
- What training does the mediator have in divorce mediation, and when was the training? How many divorce mediations have they done?
- Does the mediator help couples only with parenting arrangements or does the mediator address property and financial support issues as well?
- Is the mediator a member of the Academy of Family Mediators? If so, is the mediator a Practitioner Member?
- Does the mediator expect your attorneys to be present? If so, the mediator is probably not mediating but conducting a settlement conference.

Avoid anyone who offers to serve as both your mediator *and* as your attorney or therapist. It is an ethical conflict for professionals to take more than one professional role with the same client.

Lawyers

If your marriage is ending and you're not using mediation, you will probably need to use an attorney to help settle matters between you and your spouse. Each of you will need your own attorney. Don't use your family lawyer or your business attorney—they don't want to take sides. Don't use the lawyer who did your real estate settlement. Use an attorney whose specialty is domestic relations.

Beware of all the advice you get to hire the meanest divorce lawyer in town. The meanest lawyer won't make you feel any better and will cost you a lot. Good attorneys see their job as helping you settle matters, not extracting revenge for you. Therapists and other professionals can usually offer referrals to competent attorneys. You can also contact the Domestic Relations Committee of your local Bar Association and ask for names of competent, experienced attorneys who are low-key and are known for helping their clients settle divorce matters fairly and with as little conflict as possible. Use these criteria, too, in assessing the attorneys that your friends recommend.

Specialized Resources

Help with an affair comes in other forms as well. Check out the World Wide Web. Excellent Web sites that discuss affairs include www.affairs-help.com (my site) and www.vaughan-vaughan.com.

Twelve-step groups focusing on sexual addiction are active throughout the country. Contact Sex and Love Addicts Anonymous or Sexaholics Anonymous.

Seminars and groups addressing other types and other aspects of affairs are also available in some areas. Retreats for couples who have experienced an affair are occasionally offered. Therapists who are knowledgeable can often put you in touch with such resources.

Books can be a wonderful source of help. Check out those listed in the Recommended Reading section at the back of this book, but don't stop there. In addition to books on affairs, also read books that help you understand how your deeper wounds came to be. It's often easier to work on changing your behavior when you understand that you had good reason, given the situation you were in as a young child, for developing your behavior patterns, even though they are a big problem today.

Summary

Let yourself get the help you need. Affairs are too hot, too painful, and too complicated to tackle alone. It's no good to be Superman or Superwoman when inside you're hurting or totally confused or in some other place where the affair has you perturbed and disturbed. Good help exists. Find it, use it, and commit yourself to resolving old, troublesome issues and becoming the best you can be. You've paid too dearly for this opportunity to waste it. Make the most of it!

Chapter Ten

Talking with Your Children, Your Friends, and Your Family

Helping your children and accepting support for
yourself will ensure that your journey is not a
solitary one.

Although affairs begin in secret, the tentacles of an affair soon
reach into all the important relationships in your life: children and
family, friends and neighbors, work and community. This is true
whatever part of the triangle is yours. As the tentacles connect,
each person touched by the affair responds in some way: keeping
the secret or exposing it, feeling hurt, judging those involved, fan-
ning the flames or backing off, taking sides, relating old wives' tales,
getting even, avoiding conflict, feeling confused, and most of all,
giving advice. In reality, there is no such thing as a secret affair.

Since this is the case, we'll look at helping your children through
this crisis, and then at how to handle the tentacles of your affair that
extend into your relationships with friends, family, and community.

The Affair and Your Children

When Ron, a high school sophomore, accidentally discovered his
father's affair, his academics took a nosedive. He got an F in everything but Phys Ed, where he managed to get a D, in the semester
after he overheard his father's lovey-dovey phone conversation to
Nora. He couldn't tell his mother about the affair because she
would fall apart. If he confronted his father he was afraid his father
would just write him off, maybe even leave the family. That too

would be his fault. So Ron struggled under the weight of his father's secret. His grades became the family focus, allowing his parents to distract themselves from their marital problems.

The school counselor realized something serious was developing and referred Ron and his parents to a therapist. The therapist helped Ron's parents uncover the secret affair and begin talking together about what was really going on in their marriage. The affair was now out in the open. Even though Ron was still anxious about whether his folks would split, the burden of the secret was lifted, and he stopped feeling responsible for his parents' problems. His folks were the therapist's responsibility now. He no longer had to protect his mother, or worry about what his father would do. He could get back to his own life. His grades went back up.

A lot of parents hesitate to tell their kids about an affair in the family. They insist that the kids don't know and are doing just fine: "What they don't know, won't hurt them." They are afraid their kids can't handle knowing, that they'll be devastated, that their grades will go down. They also feel ashamed and worry that telling the truth will irretrievably damage their relationship with the child. Others, usually obsessive spouses who have been dumped via an Exit Affair, will assert that children should know everything, down to the minute details of the affair itself. They insist that the children should know how untrustworthy and awful the other parent is.

Both approaches are seriously flawed. The first withholds information that enables children to put in perspective the emotional and behavioral changes in their family. Kids worry when they experience tension or feel changes in the family but don't understand what is going on. The legacy of family secrets is difficulty trusting those close to you. Tony, whose mother's affair was hidden from him for years, commented sadly, "You never know the real truth." The opposite approach sets the children up to take sides in a fight that is not theirs. This can cost them their childhood, their relationship with a parent, and the ability to form an intimate relationship as an adult. There is a middle ground and it's based on what your kids need: age appropriate information that omits judgments or appeals to take sides.

The Golden Rules

- Talk to your friends about your hurt, anger, and frustrations— not to your kids. Do so only when your children are not around, even when you think they can't hear or are not listening (because they are).

- Listen to your kids. Listening to your kids does not mean soliciting their advice, it means listening to their feelings. It helps if someone is listening to you and your feelings, so that you are not totally depleted when you're talking with your kids.

Typical Reactions of Children to a Hidden Affair

A parent's affair is always a problem when it is not dealt with appropriately in the family. When the affair is not addressed, the children experience it as a betrayal, much as the spouse does. In addition, kids are caught in the dysfunctional family dynamics ensuing from the affair. Everyone does better when the family addresses this crisis openly.

Typical reactions of children when an affair is hidden from them or from the other parent include the following:

- *Silence.* The child doesn't say anything (which parents want to read as the kids aren't being affected). Kids know when they don't have your permission to talk about something. They don't ask—instead they may hassle you about a different issue, one that's safer to talk about.

- *Acting out behavior.* Kids' misbehavior often indicates they are experiencing a problem that's beyond their coping ability. In the case of a parental affair, the child's misbehavior usually starts suddenly. Matt got into a series of driving mishaps, including two accidents and several tickets, before his parents became aware that this was a cry for help and that it was linked to his father's ongoing affair. A parent's job is to find out what a child's misbehavior means, and to get help in doing so when that is necessary.

- *Loyalty conflicts.* These often show up as depression or stomachaches or other physical complaints.

- *Being too good.* Kids who adopt this strategy have taken on responsibility for trying to fix things and prevent disaster. They may believe that they are the cause of any parental discord.

- *Attempts to protect a parent.* A child becomes oversolicitous of the parent perceived as weaker, or takes sides with the parent who is seeking an ally.

- *Escaping.* Kids spend time elsewhere trying to escape the tension or to avoid tripping over the hidden elephant.

- *Self-destructive behavior.* Kids will even get self-destructive if that's what it takes to get problems out in the open.

Talking to Your Children About the Affair

Once the affair has been revealed to your spouse it's time for the two of you to talk to your children about what is going on. Plan for this carefully, and do it together. Put your own feelings about the affair aside when talking to your kids. They will appreciate it now and forever.

How you talk to your kids is critical. Kids often hear either too much about a parent's affair or too little. The child who hears too much starts taking care of the parent, either being the confidant of the betraying parent or the defender of the betrayed parent.

Kids don't fare much better in families where no one talks. Kids are always aware of the emotional pitch of the household, and any changes in it. Knowing that something is going on, without getting any real information, is confusing at best. Without facts to explain the tension and with no one to talk to, kids are stuck finding other ways to deal with the situation on their own.

The tiniest kids, babies and toddlers, will feel the tension but words will not work. These kids need physical reassurance, such as being held and soothed by each parent and by others who love them. They also need a decrease in the tensions. Children from four to seven have no conception of an affair. They might be told simply that Dad is upset because Mom is spending a lot of time with Mr. Smith. Eight- to eleven-year-olds may have some vague idea of what an affair is, but it is probably sufficient to tell them the same thing that the younger kids are told. Junior high school age and up will understand the meaning of an affair. They need to be told the truth, preferably by both of you together, in the simplest terms. Dad might say, for example, "I'm involved in an affair with a woman at work." Chances are the adolescent has already figured it out.

The problem with saying this much to your children is that it changes your children's perception of you. Normally, children grow up viewing their parents as asexual. Telling children of a parent's affair means children are faced with the fact that their parents are sexual beings, long before they are ready for this. However, if *anyone* else knows about the affair, if there is the *slightest* chance a child might hear about it, or the parent is living with the third party, the children need to hear about the affair from their parents. You can prevent the additional betrayal of allowing your child to bump into the affair accidentally.

Be prepared to talk to your children about what you are doing to address the situation. Tell them whether you are actively working on the marriage, if a separation is in the offing or not, and whether you're in therapy. If you don't know yet what's going to happen, you can say just that, but make sure you reassure your children that you and your spouse will continue to parent them.

It's all too easy for kids to be caught in the conflict and craziness of a parent's affair. Your kids may feel betrayed by the affair, much like you or your spouse. They need help in coming to terms with what's going on in your family. Kids do better when the family addresses this crisis openly. In other words, once there is an affair, what matters most for your kids is *how* the affair is dealt with.

More Golden Rules that your kids need you to honor:

- Give your kids honest information, preferably from both of you together. If your spouse absolutely refuses to talk to the kids, and nothing you or the kids say changes anything, then you need to do the talking—but for your kids' sake, you've got to do it without making your spouse the bad guy. Again, consider asking a counselor to guide you.

- Choose your timing carefully. Thanksgiving day, the child's birthday, or right before an exam or an important game is not the time. Neither is the day before one of you leaves town on a business trip or the child leaves for camp. While there is no good time, there are better times.

- Make the information fit the child's age. The truth means different things at different ages. Little kids don't have any concept of an affair. They can understand, "Mom's upset with Dad because he's spending a lot of time with Mrs. Jones and Mom misses him." Teens are very aware of what *affair* means. If you need professional help to plan and carry this out, get it.

- Let your children talk to you about feeling scared or angry. They need what we all need: someone (in this case their parents) to hear, respect, and acknowledge their feelings.

Betty told her teenage daughter that she had been involved in an affair and had just ended it. She went on to say, "Now, I don't want you to be upset about this." Her daughter, Pam, responded by getting angry. Pam experienced Betty's remark as uncaring, as dismissive, as asking Pam to erase her feelings so Betty wouldn't feel guilty. Betty tried again, declaring, "Everything will be OK." Pam got angrier, trying to get her mother to hear how she felt. Contrast this with Dennis's acknowledgment of his son's anger: "I know that you're very angry at me." His son felt heard, said, "Yes, I am," and calmed down.

- Give your children a status report on what is happening to the marriage. Are you committed to it, working on it, or is it over? If you don't know in which direction you're going, tell your kids just that—it's better than the guessing and worrying that they do when they're kept in the dark.

- Tell your children if separation is imminent. They won't like hearing it—but they need to know.

- Whatever you do, spare your kids a fight over custody. Forget the idea that since he has a lover, you'll keep the kids. This protection against abandonment doesn't help anyone. Your kids need you both. They also need you to consider *their* needs, and they need you to minimize your conflict.[1] For guidance on how to do well by your children, no matter how you feel about each other, read *Mom's House, Dad's House* by Isolina Ricci.[2] Strongly consider using divorce mediation rather than litigation in making your decisions about parenting (and for finances and property too) to keep the level of conflict low.

- Tell your kids if you're seeing a counselor or therapist. It takes the burden off your kids to know that someone else is helping you work on your problems. Talk with the counselor about whether a family session might be helpful for the kids.

- Free your kids to love both parents and be loyal to both of you. Refrain from asking them to take sides, be your confidants, comfort you, spy, or in any other way carry responsibility for either or both of you. If you do this, your kids will be eternally grateful (although they won't tell you until much later).

Children's Reactions to Learning About a Parent's Affair

How do kids react to learning that a parent is having an affair? Kids' reactions vary with their ages, the type of affair, the nature and duration of the problems in the family, the level of conflict, and the ability of the parents to parent. Many kids are disappointed, especially if they've had the betraying parent on a pedestal. Others are angry, especially older teenagers and young adults who are struggling with their own sexuality and relationships. Some kids are relieved that a parent who's been grossly unappreciated by the other parent over the years is finally finding some happiness. Younger kids, with no ability to understand the word *affair*, experience the tension and conflict in the family. Most kids are worried about what's going to happen to them and their family.

When a parent falls off the pedestal it changes children's whole conception of who their family is and thus, their sense of who they are. They attempt to fill gaps in the family, taking care of a parent, or of younger sibs. They try to push the family back into the shape it used to be in.

Remember Doug and Janie in Chapter Seven, who were struggling with a Split Self Affair? Their daughter, Katie, was a high school senior and their son, Kevin, a college sophomore when their mother tearfully told them about their father's affair. Katie became very solicitous of her mother, trying to make her feel better. Kevin got furious at his father, and told his mother that he wasn't going to speak to his father unless his father made the right decision. Doug responded by laying low. These kids were pulled back into the middle of their parents' relationship, just at the time they were moving out into the world. The affair called into question the values and expectations they were relying on to guide them as they left home. That's why Kevin was so angry—the props had been knocked out from under him. Katie, still at home, found herself taking responsibility for mothering her mother—not the best task for her senior year (or any other).

Children are worried about what will happen next. Who will care for them if their parents separate? Who will care for the abandoned parent? Embarrassment is a big factor: parents aren't supposed to act like this. For the duration of the betrayed spouse's obsession, kids may need support from other adults, until the parents are able to get back to parenting. Sometimes family therapy is useful in getting the family talking. After an affair, parents have to rebuild trust with their children, as well as with each other, by taking responsibility for their own behavior.

Children of Sexual Addicts, where chaos and unpredictability are the family norm, have an especially difficult time with parental affairs. The Addict's affairs are seldom hidden, and there may be a sexual undercurrent in the family. The parent who is sexually addicted usually has other addictions as well. Kids are abused, neglected, and taught "Don't think, don't feel, and don't tell." They experience the emotional emptiness of the parents and have to cope with the dysfunctional family behaviors. These kids may take responsibility for being the parent in the family or they may follow in the footsteps of their parents. In either case, shame is a big presence.

These children need help from an adult outside the family— someone who can provide emotional support and comfort plus guidance in how to deal with the family's problems. This might be a relative or friend who sees and understands the problems the child is facing, a school counselor, a coach, a therapist, or a twelve-step group of some sort. Ideally, the parents will also get help with their own problems and be better equipped to help their children. However, of couples experiencing an affair, Sexual Addicts and their spouses are the most likely to deny they need help. Even when these parents get help, it will be some time before the benefits spill over to their children. Thus, help from outside is necessary for children of Sexual Addicts.

How You Can Ease Your Children's Pain and Bewilderment

Children are like little sponges, picking up any and all nuances of tension in the family. They know when you're hurting, and may try to fix it for you. They are bewildered by what is happening and worried about what is going to happen. You can offer them reassurance and nurturing in many ways, even with an affair in the background.

- Show your love with a hug, a pat, encouraging words, snuggle time, a bit of humor.
- Make your reassurance tangible by demonstrating that you and your spouse can cooperate in being parents.

- Keep your normal routines going. They provide security and predictability.

- Make it easy for your children to share with you their fears and anxieties about what is happening. Comment on nonverbal messages, such as being very quiet, and invite the child to talk about what is bothering him or her.

- Don't tell your child to be brave, or make false promises, trying to make it better. Instead, take your child's pain, fear, or tears seriously. Offer a hug, kind words, a listening ear.

- Be aware that your child may need some special attention from each of you during this difficult period. You'll be more able to meet your kids' needs if you are feeling heard yourself.

- Arrange for your child to spend special time with other adults that your child loves. Make these visits short so that your child doesn't worry about what is happening to you in his or her absence.

- If your marriage is ending, find books about divorce that the children can read or that you can read to them.

Essentially you want to reassure your children by your behavior that both of you will continue to be parents, that they won't lose either of you, and that whatever happens, you will be there with them, helping them work it out. Conveying the attitude that all of you will be able to handle this difficult and painful situation is very reassuring, and it provides a positive example of handling life's adversities.

Children, the Exit Affair, and the Affair Partner

Dan and Jody separated recently after he told Jody he was leaving her for Ellen. This is their first "discussion" about the children's contact with Ellen.

> *Jody:* How could you do a thing like that—taking the children to see that woman! I don't want my children exposed to her!

Dan: The kids like Ellen. She's good to them.

Jody: It's one thing for you and your sneaking, cheating self to be with that tramp—but you're not going to take my kids to see her!

Dan: They're my kids too, and I'll decide who they see when they're with me!

Child: (wails) Mommyyyy. . . .

Sound familiar? This is an all-too-common occurrence when an affair is used to end the marriage. The dumped spouse is enraged at being replaced by the third party. Kids are pulled into the middle of this volatile triangle when they are involved prematurely with the third party. Fights ensue, which the children overhear. It doesn't have to be this way.

When the marriage ends and the affair continues, kids need protected space before having to interact with the affair partner. It's not that the third party is a secret, but that your kids need time to grieve, to share feelings of disappointment and anger that their family as they've known it is ending, and to adjust to the new family situation before having to incorporate the third party into their lives. Additional losses, such as moving away from friends, must also be grieved. When all is going well in the divorce process, your kids need at least six months to a year to grieve and to adjust to all these changes. It is important that kids have this time for themselves, unencumbered by having to make room in the family for the third party—or parental fights about the third party.

Consider making a pact with each other that the kids will have no contact with any new partner for six months. When the six months is up, determine whether the kids are ready to meet the affair partner, or any other new partner. If so, plan for gradual contact with the new partner, not total immersion. If the kids are not ready, identify how much longer they will need. Any extension needs to be based on the children's needs, not on a spouse's neediness or jealousy or on the affair partner's insistence on being acknowledged.

Effects of Parental Affairs in Adult Life

Sometimes children don't have the opportunity to resolve the issues about their parent's affair until they are grown. In my research with adults whose parents had affairs when they were children, they reported difficulties with secrecy, their ability to trust, unresolved anger and pain, disregard for their own feelings, family schisms, relationship problems, and confused boundaries. They needed to resolve questions about the past, to confirm intuitions, to put the pieces of their personal history in place.

Beth, age twenty-eight, observed, "All the difficulties in our family came together around the affair," which occurred when she was sixteen, "but we couldn't talk about it. My family never experienced any intimacy—that's what I had to learn to do on my own." These days she feels split. She wants to protect her mother, but her mother complains that she is not supported by her kids since they have a relationship with their father and he is living with his affair partner. "My mother was totally preoccupied with being wronged, and she's still vengeful." About her father, Beth says, "I don't trust him—he's good at deceiving. I could never trust what I heard. There was the seed of deception from the beginning. Now is the time I think we can handle talking about it." She has started talking to her brothers and sisters about a family session for this purpose.

With issues of trust and secrecy, these "adult kids" tend to go to one extreme or the other. Tom declared, "If I find someone has lied, they're dead to me." Barbara has concluded, "You can never be certain of who to believe or what's true." Meg, the daughter of a sexual addict, describes her evolution: "I used to be able to keep stuff in different compartments. I laughed and talked a lot—but I didn't let anybody in. It cost me a lot—a lot of tragic mistakes. Sometimes I feel like I'm made of glass, and I'm about to shatter." At the other end of the spectrum is Hugh, who describes himself as an open book, telling everything to anyone.

"I lost respect for my father. Not because he had the affair—but because of the way he handled it," reported Jerry. "I was alienated from him until I was in my thirties, when I began to understand his motivations." Ivan, who as a teen suspected his mother's affair but whose family never talked about it, said: "My mother finally told me some of the details when my marriage was falling apart. It helped me put the pieces in place."

Anger is common, even now, many years later. Much of the anger is at feeling so helpless. The anger is not just toward the parent having the affair but also at the other parent who didn't deal with the affair effectively and who underfunctioned as a parent or as a spouse. Eva reported, "I couldn't understand Mother putting up with it."

Fran, the daughter of a sexual addict, confided: "My own temper frightens me. I cope tremendously, then I go over the edge, and I lay it all with all the details on the other person." Her rage makes her physically sick, and she trembles and vomits. "I know I'm overreacting, and it's scary, but I don't know how else to deal with the pain." She is proud of never crying in front of her father—but now she still cannot cry. She insists her rage is not for what happened to her but "for what he did to my mother and little sister. There was so much lying. I think that hurt me the most."

Carole realized at the age of thirty-five that how she felt about her mother didn't affect her mother at all, but it was destroying Carole. She decided to make her mother die in her mind, and then she grieved over her mother's death.

Another woman reported that, "Until I was grown, I always thought that it was what he did to mother. . . . It wasn't just mother." In contrast, a few women put their mother on a pedestal for having coped with so much.

Loss was always close to the surface. Bert said sadly, "My father's affair meant I lost my father—I only saw him twice while I was growing up." Marianne proclaimed, "I was very hurt. If he cared enough about me he would have stopped seeing her. It didn't have anything to do with how he treated my mother. I spent my whole life trying to be Daddy's Little Girl, and he doesn't remember the day I was born." Not surprisingly, she picked men who didn't like most women, but who liked her and thought she was different. She is revising this strategy because she's twice divorced.

Most wanted to live life differently from their parents and to some extent were succeeding. Would they replicate their parent's affair? Some were sure they would never have an affair. Others had already had an affair, or their spouse had, and they were sorting out the aftermath. In most cases they saw the connection between their affair or their spouse's and unfinished issues from childhood, particularly the underlying issues related to their parent's affair.

Alex has mixed emotions about the aftereffects of his father's affair: "I was very uncomfortable with the kind of relationship my mother wanted" (companion and confidant). "Partly I feel like I was treated unfairly, but another part of me knows that's how I became the person I am, and I like being a caring person."

A different perspective comes from Nancy, whose father was an alcoholic, "I'm glad to know my mother had some fun—at least I hope she did."

Reactions to the third party varied. It was easier when the affair did not result in marriage. Susan said she was angry at her father's affair partner, but not at the woman her father met later. Ray described his stepmother who had been the third party as the "stereotype of the Wicked Witch of the West. She didn't care about anybody but herself, not even my father." In contrast are success stories like Allison's. Her family had worked hard to overcome the aftermath of her father's affair. Allison paid tribute to the work her family did when she told her stepmother (who had been the third party), "I feel badly about my mother being hurt, but if it hadn't happened, I wouldn't have you."

The "adult kids" in this study are unanimous in their belief that having someone to talk to would have helped. Their comments:

"There should be a time the kids should know. I think mostly the kids know. I'm glad I knew—I wish there had been nothing to know."

"If my stepfather had held me close, told me it wasn't right, and somehow fixed it—or told me he was working on it. I needed someone to talk to about it."

"Tell the child to call the hotline—it's safe; it's someone that doesn't know you. It has to be someone safe."

"If I'd had someone to talk to, they could have provided assurance. If they confirmed there was a problem, I wouldn't have felt so responsible. If a therapist had said, 'Your parents have made some mistakes—they're here for help and I'll help them,' it would have been very reassuring. Instead, nobody was talking."

Ginger's advice to parents is, "Be honest! Accept the heat from your kids. They're going to be angry. They have the right to know what intimately affects them."

The bottom line is talk to your kids about what is happening in your family, and do so in a way that isn't damaging. Be available to listen to their concerns and fears, be honest in what you say, and don't give them the responsibility for your feelings. They will be upset, but they will be grateful for your honesty and your support.

Friends, Family, Work, and Community

Marriages are embedded in a larger fabric of kids, friends, family, and community. This network of relationships sustains us, frustrates us, and is both a joy and a burden. These relationships are based on sharing an important aspect of life, whether it be school experiences, military duty, interests, genes, children's ages, or the like. Our connections with these people run the gamut from narrow and temporary to intense and lifelong. Generally we believe that those we are closest to share similar values and behave in similar ways.

An affair is akin to a collision for those close by. It is unexpected (at least to some degree), and generally outside the norms of daily life. It is threatening, and the more unexpected the affair and the closer the friends and family, the greater the threat. At the same time it is titillating, like a good soap opera or a romance novel, except here friends and family have a front row seat. They can even get in on the act.

What's Behind Your Friends' and Relatives' Reactions

Let's take a look at what's behind the reactions of many of your friends and relatives. Affairs ruffle everyone's feathers. For friends and family, just as for the spouse, it is the betrayal, rather than the sex, that is so threatening. Learning about the affair in your life is going to trigger emotional reactions in many of them. Factors that shape their responses include personal experience with an affair (their own or someone close), beliefs about marriage and about men and women, their coping styles, and their own fears. They may get angry, be curious, take sides, or disappear, but most often they give advice—giving advice is a way of not feeling so helpless.

You'll hear a chorus of well-meant recommendations and admonitions: "How can you put up with it! I would never put up with it if my husband cheated on me!" "If my wife cheated on me, she'd be gone!" "Throw the jerk out!" "Clean out the bank accounts." "Get a private detective and get the goods on her." "You better talk to my attorney!" In the background, tabloids speculate on whether divorce is in the offing for the latest famous name found to be involved in an affair and the talk shows question whether it's possible to get over an affair. Don't give in to all the advice to be vindictive. It will help the advice-givers feel in control, but it won't buy you anything but trouble.

You are the one who needs to be in charge of decisions about your life right now, and you need to make your decisions for the right reasons: your reasons. You can prevent future problems by thinking about how you want to handle the affair within your network of relationships, rather than just reacting. Consciously deciding gives you more control.

Talking About the Affair in Your Life

You do need to talk about the affair in your life. But not to just anyone. If you keep your wits about you early on, it's possible for you to decide who to talk to, when to open up, and what to say. If you and your mate are communicating, you can decide together who gets let in and who doesn't. If the two of you aren't talking, it's still important for you to make careful decisions about who you talk to. Once you get good emotional support, you'll be in a better place for talking to your kids.

Basic principles for talking:

- Choose carefully who you *want* to confide in.
- Determine who you *need* to talk with to prevent worse consequences.
- Ask for the kind of support you want.
- Ignore all the advice that comes your way, well-meant or not, and reserve the right to make your own decisions.

Two factors have a bearing on who you talk to: who is affected by the affair, and who you choose to look to for support. With friends and family, you don't owe information to anyone but your spouse and your kids. Anybody else should be chosen carefully. With work and community, who you talk to and what you say depends on whether and how the overflow from the affair has reached those parts of your life.

Thinking About Talking to Your Family

Most people don't want to tell their parents about their own affair. The idea of telling parents elicits shame and embarrassment, and the specter of being inundated with critical advice or "woe is me." Many don't want to tell their parents about a partner's affair either, at least not at first. As for telling your partner's parents about his or her affair, resist the temptation. You're into blame and punishment and it won't make you look or feel good. The affair is essentially an issue between you and your spouse, not a football for the family to kick around.

The wisdom of telling your own parents early on about your spouse's affair depends on your motivation. Are you looking to be declared blameless, seeking allies for revenge, or are your parents truly good friends who will support you? Good friends can be defined as accepting, comforting, and non-blaming. A judgment call needs to be made about what's to be gained and how great is the cost of telling your parents, or of not telling them. Ask yourself the following questions to get a reading on your situation:

- Are you able to talk to your parents in a way that will get you some support?
- Are your parents capable of offering emotional support given their feelings about betrayal?
- In other words, can your parents still love and comfort you even if they don't approve of what is happening?
- Can they keep from jumping on the blame bandwagon?
- Is this the right time to talk with them?
- Are your parents about to learn of the affair from someone else?
- Do you and your spouse need to resolve some things first?

Any no answers to the first six questions or a yes to the seventh mean slow down and reconsider.

Abigail's situation illustrates the difficulties that some families have with an affair. Abigail is from a family that gets together fairly often but no one talks about problems or emotions, other than to complain. She and her husband, Brent, don't talk either. A few months ago Abigail got involved with a man at work. Her situation got out of control in a hurry after Brent discovered the affair. In a fit of anger he disclosed it to Jan, Abigail's sister. On learning of the affair, Jan is startled. "What do you know! Abigail has this whole secret life. She's not who I thought she is. I wonder what else she's holding out from me. Does Dad know about this yet?" And then she considers the flip side: "If Abigail can do this, anyone can. Could this happen to me? Maybe there are things I don't really know. Maybe I take things too much for granted. But *my* husband wouldn't ever do anything like this. We've got a good marriage." So

Jan gets busy decreasing the threat. How? By telling others what is going on and giving advice to Abigail. It keeps Jan a step removed from her own anxiety.

Abigail's mom is horrified when Jan tells her about the affair—it makes her wonder where she went wrong as a parent. She keeps it from Abigail's dad, so that he won't get upset and difficult. Besides, he had an affair a number of years ago and she doesn't want to have to remember that. So she offers advice to make up for any lack of parenting in the past and to avoid her own pain from the past. (It's not hard to see how Abigail became a Conflict Avoider!) By this time, family dynamics are up and running in ways that will create additional difficulties for Abigail and Brent.

Assessing Your Family. Before reading further, take a moment to consider how Abigail's situation would play out in your own family, and identify the danger points.

- What might your family do that would interfere with keeping your options open?
- How will the gossiping and secret-keeping affect you?
- What do you want in the way of support from family members? Are they capable of offering it? How can you coach them?
- What advice will you get? Do you want it?
- What emotional support will you get, and from whom? False assurances that everything will be fine don't help when you know your life is coming apart.

Among your options is choosing not to tell either set of parents or other family members, or to tell only selected family. Trustworthy brothers and sisters can be valuable sounding boards when there's an affair. In some ways they know you better than anyone else.

Once you are clear about what you want, you can decide who you are going to tell and how. The basic rules are keep it simple, say how you're feeling, and indicate what kind of support you want. They'll probably want to know whether your marriage is on or off. Perfectly acceptable answers include "I don't know," and "I don't even want to think about that right now." Remember that no matter who you tell and what you say, the big decisions belong to you and your spouse.

Carl, who began an affair four months ago, confided to his brother, "I need to talk to you about something that's got me feeling awful. I want you to promise me you won't tell anyone. I'm having an affair with a woman at work. I don't quite know how I got into it, and I don't know how to get out of it—or if I even want to get out of it. It's driving me nuts! I've got to be able to talk to someone about it until I get myself straight." Carl's wife may be upset that family members knew before she did, but if Carl's brother helps him move toward telling her, this should not be a problem.

Special Problems. The consequences of some affairs are especially traumatic, poisoning family relationships, damaging lives, and creating family schisms. These are the affairs that break an additional taboo: the affair is with a family member, or the affair results in the birth of a child.

An affair with a family or stepfamily member presents major difficulties. The pain of this double betrayal is so intense that the marriage seldom survives, and family relationships are damaged as well. It feels like incest, and sends shock waves throughout the family. Woody Allen's affair with his adopted stepdaughter resulted in a traumatic and messy split-up with Mia Farrow, and permanent damage to his reputation. The emotional consequences for his stepdaughter–affair partner and for the other children are yet to be tallied. Waste no time in getting professional help if you're in this situation.

Few marriages survive when a child is born of the affair. Many such pregnancies are accidental. Those that are deliberate are usually designed to compel a hesitant affair partner to leave his wife and marry the pregnant third party. Because the child is a tangible living reminder of the betrayal, it's impossible for the affair to be totally relegated to the past. Given the enormity of this betrayal and the likelihood of continuing ties with the third party and the new child, the wife is not likely to have the strength or the desire to work toward rebuilding the marriage.

Occasionally the parentage of such a child is hidden and the marriage continues along. It's rare, however, that the child is totally hidden—although it may be years before the truth comes out. Bill disclosed that he thinks he has a half-brother, the son of a woman that his father spent a lot of time with and who looks just like Bill and his sister.

Talking to Your Friends

Whether it's your affair or your mate's you need a trusted friend to talk to. If you don't have family you can talk to, it's even more essential to have a trusted friend in whom to confide. The best people for this are not judgmental. They won't take sides but will comfort you when you're in pain and confront you when you need a push. They are people who can keep a confidence. When you're thinking about telling a friend, ask yourself the same questions recommended earlier for assessing which family members you might safely talk to.

Once you decide who to talk to, see if you can talk about what you are experiencing, not just what awful thing your spouse is doing now. Sharing your pain and your confusion with someone who cares about you will be much more satisfying than blaming. For you, feeling heard and understood is the best support of all, much better than merely taking your side. It also gives you the opportunity to hear yourself. If your friends start giving advice, help them understand that you want them to keep listening but you're not ready for advice. The best thing your friends can do is listen to you without giving advice.

Work and Community

Outside the close circle of family and friends are work relationships and community ties. Many affairs begin at work, sometimes as friendships and sometimes as sexual flings. Affair partners often get so caught up in their romantic fantasy life that they are oblivious to its effect on colleagues and office routines. You may insist that your colleagues don't know, but it's rare that they are unaware of an office affair. The "secret" has a wide impact on the entire workplace. Office jokes cover up discomfort and annoyance at work not done, at favoritism, at your unreality, at the undertow of the secret, and at the spillover from the affair itself, such as when the spouse confronts the affair partner in the office. Christie, who works in an office with forty-five employees, said, "When someone's involved in an affair at work, I just back off. They aren't able to hear anything and it gets pretty crazy."

So what can you do? Your coworkers don't want to get caught up in your deception. They will resent picking up your responsibilities or covering for you. When your spouse suspects or knows of your affair, your office may become the scene of surveillance. This puts your colleagues on the spot, and will not endear you to them, unless you are colluding in covering for each other. It should go without saying that you shouldn't spend company time on your affair.

Talking to your boss before your boss talks to you may be in order. Or, if your affair has acquired a messy trail, such as phone inquiries or stalking incidents from a jealous spouse, you will need to talk to your boss about it promptly. If you are the boss and it's your affair, get help from an outside consultant.

Be aware that in the work environment, sexual harassment charges are sometimes brought by the disgruntled party when an affair ends. Military policy prohibits extramarital affairs. Violations can result in being discharged, especially when the affair is with a subordinate. Some private companies have similar policies prohibiting sexual or secret relationships between work colleagues, even unmarried colleagues. The company is attempting to prevent claims of sexual harassment, misuse of office time and resources, vulnerability to blackmail, or even potential violence. It's common for companies to require one of the affair partners to transfer to another part of the company or look for a job elsewhere. Even though work is a prime place to get acquainted with an affair partner, and maybe because of that, you can expect to see more companies establish policies to protect themselves against the risk of office affairs.

Similar problems develop when affairs emerge in church congregations, community organizations, or other such groups. Rifts and rivalries develop easily in such an environment. Again, identify who is confronted with the fallout of your affair and what needs to be addressed with whom. The ramifications are much the same as in business except you aren't at risk of losing your job.

Summary

The affair in your life touches many people. It's important to talk to your children honestly and respectfully in a manner consistent with their age. Pay attention to their responses, both verbal and nonverbal, so that they feel free to come to you with their concerns. With friends and relatives, choose carefully who you turn to for support. You can politely ignore all the unsolicited advice that comes your way, well-meant or not, and reserve the right to make your own decisions as you rebuild your life.

Chapter Eleven

Examining the Single
Side of the Triangle

*Loneliness drove you to the affair, but now you're
more alone than ever. What can you learn that
allows you to be fully yourself with someone else?*

"What's a nice single person like me doing having an affair with
someone who is married?" wondered Susan. "It's not my style!" For
people like Susan who find themselves in an affair the answer is
rarely as simple as falling in love. Just as for the married person
in an affair, underlying emotional issues are an important part
of why you choose an affair rather than a relationship with someone who is fully available. An affair allows you to get certain
emotional needs met while limiting your emotional investment, at
least initially.

Some affairs that singles enter into are brief interludes or one-
night stands with a minimal investment of time and emotion;
others grow into serious relationships. Being the other woman or
the other man can be an important but temporary way-station, as
in the first year after ending a marriage, or it can become a way
of life, as with a serious long-term affair or a string of sexual
liaisons.

Different issues underlie each of these patterns. They include a
fear of intimacy (married people are "safe"), the validation derived
from a conquest, the pursuit of romantic fantasies, the fear of
becoming dependent, or the need to numb internal pain.

Serious Affairs

Many serious affairs begin as good friendships. You already have rapport. When you add loneliness and a case of boundary drift, you've got an affair. Early in a serious affair, the romance and excitement run high for both of you. Forgotten dreams spring to life; the promise of feeling alive is in the air, and the fantasy of being whole and complete with your married lover seems within reach. It's your secret—just the two of you—and it's delicious. You put other concerns aside as you embark on this adventure.

It feels wonderful to have someone want you and want to be with you, to hold you and touch you. Not only do you feel loved, the affair makes you feel lovable—and maybe more important, allows you to feel able to love again. Finally, there is passion in your life! It's overpowering and irresistible. It doesn't matter what other people think, you say to yourself, although you also give the affair a low profile.

The serious affairs that singles enter into are the Split Self triangle and the Exit Affair. These are the most emotionally rewarding affairs for singles, but the rewards come with a price.

The Split Self Affair and You

Single women are more willing to invest in long-term affairs with Split Selves than are single men. Being the third party in these affairs is not easy. Your married partner is still attached to his marriage and family by ties of obligation if not affection. He struggles with whether to choose you or choose his spouse; with whether or not to end the marriage. The attachment to you is through his emotions. You represent his dreams of emotional passion, of feeling alive, of being free of the obligation to sacrifice himself for the good of others. He has you cast in the role of the all-giving, all-loving partner who makes him feel alive and whole.

Your lover fits your dreams as well. He takes care of you in a way that you've always wanted but probably never had. He is solicitous, buys you luxuries you can't afford to buy for yourself, takes you on "business trips" to romantic places, and builds up your self-esteem. (He is a caretaker, that hasn't changed! The only change is that he's caretaking you and not his wife.) You look up to him and defer to his judgment, his choices—and his schedule. You feel empowered by his need and desire for you. It feels wonderful to be the chosen one, to be put on a pedestal, to be revered as the salvation to your affair partner's problems. You too feel alive with him. You're the one he says he can talk to, not like his wife.

He draws word pictures of your future together, promising, "As soon as Johnny finishes high school—" or "When the summer is over—" he will end his marriage. He describes his wife as uncaring, critical, and demanding, and it's just a matter of time before things are sufficiently in order for him to end the marriage and then the two of you will be able to be together. For a while this is enough. Gradually, though, you begin to realize that he is not leaving his marriage, and you start pressing him to do so. He provides reasons for delaying: the kids, the finances, his wife's shaky emotional state, after the holidays, and so on. Time piles up and one day you realize you've invested a year, two years, five years, or more.

It's easy to dream about the future from the safety of the secret—your delicious and intense passion is not yet offset by the daily demands of living together. There's a cost, however. Betsy remarked, "I love him, but I have a real hard time when he goes home to his wife night after night, month after month, year after year." For others, the disturbing moments are when your anticipated get-together is disrupted by last-minute changes in the plans of your affair partner's spouse, or by the needs of his kids. Despite the most favored status he gives you verbally, you're not fully comfortable. Sometimes you're downright lonely.

By choosing a Split Self as your partner, you limit yourself. You've taken yourself out of the running for someone who is truly available and joined the ranks of those who fear down deep that they're not good enough or desirable enough to be fully loved, or who fear being swallowed up by a partner's needs. You wait alone for your lover to find time to be with you, you come second when there are family demands, you're in a stagnant competition with his spouse, and you are a participant in the dishonesty and betrayal of the affair. You don't feel good about it, but you too attempt to justify the situation: "He needs me—his wife is just so difficult," or "That marriage is long since over—it's just a matter of getting the legal stuff in order," or "We keep each other going. He gets some needs met with me that he doesn't get at home. He's probably much better at home because of it."

Kendra is typical of the many single women who become seriously involved with married men. Divorced, widowed, or never married, they choose a partner who is not fully available. They live their lives on the sidelines while dreaming about the future.

"He is such a good person," says Kendra, describing her fifty-five-year-old married lover. "As soon as he can get a divorce, we're going to get married. . . . Only his wife won't give him a divorce. She's just using him. You should hear how awful she's been . . . he's been a saint to put up with so much—and all for the sake of his children." Kendra, who is thirty-two and single, admits she has Paul on a pedestal. When Paul can't get away to be with her, she spends her time planning for their future together. The danger for Kendra is that she will stay with Paul for so long that she closes off many of life's opportunities, such as having children of her own.

The Making of a Split Self Affair Partner. Divided parents often unwittingly set the stage for the role of the Other Woman. Children who are forced to choose one parent over the other are caught in a double bind. If a daughter chooses her mother, she learns to view men with suspicion. If she chooses her father, she is essentially competing with her mother. If her father responds by turning to her rather than to her mother, she is the Other Woman. The experience of beating out mother and getting the goodies from dad is so powerful and so seductive that few daughters who are chosen by their fathers can resist. This is a common dynamic in dysfunctional families, both intact and divorced.

Bonnie describes herself as being a loving woman who is attentive to the needs of Bernie, a married man with whom she has been involved for the last three years. She thought Bernie would be out of his marriage before this, but his wife is giving him an awful time and he doesn't want his kids to get hurt. He did move out for a few days, but he felt so guilty about the kids he moved back home.

What Bonnie hasn't looked at yet is her pattern of picking unavailable men. She chalks it up to happenstance but it's more than that. Bonnie is replaying the oedipal triangle. As a kid, Bonnie was her father's favorite, even favored over her mother. She paid for that "privilege" by being the focus of her mother's harsh criticism and cutting innuendo. Bonnie's legacy is twofold: a misplaced need to keep some distance from the man she loves so that it's not incest (she really doesn't want to *win* her father—she wanted her parents to love her and let her be a kid), and anger at her mother for being so critical. She views Bernie's wife from that perspective.

The original "affair" started with Bonnie's parents. Her father substituted Bonnie for Bonnie's mother, instead of working out his problems with his wife. Bonnie's mother got mad at Bonnie instead of working out her problems with her husband. In Bonnie's current affair with Bernie she is repeating the same pattern, trying in some abstract, radar-like way to work it out so that she can finish growing up. Instead of competing with her mother, she's substituted Bernie's wife. Her conscious hope is that Bernie will fully choose her. Unconsciously she's afraid of being dependent, of needing too much from "dad," of giving up her own life the way she did as a child. At the same time she feels guilty about competing with her mother, and at an unconscious level believes she deserves to be punished. Being with an unavailable man is part punishment and part protection. It keeps Bonnie from being totally vulnerable but it gets in the way of feeling truly intimate and secure.

Bonnie is able to be emotionally present with Bernie because she always has an escape. If Bernie actually leaves his wife, Bonnie may be hard-put: she won't be able to keep the kind of distance from "dad" that she's desired and this will be scary. Moreover, being the everyday partner rather than having a special and privileged status changes the relationship. There are more demands and expectations, more issues about the daily business of life. It's not so romantic. Bernie might even grow to see her in much the way he views his wife today. Judith Viorst describes this dilemma very well: "The only man worth having . . . is a man who has been stolen from somebody else. But sometimes the stealing is valued more than the prize. Sometimes the beating-out-mother part is the most important part of the oedipal fantasy: If a man will leave his wife for you, it proves you're a better woman than his wife. Except when he leaves, you may no longer want him."[1]

Bonnie's work is to break free of her parents' triangle, give up her pursuit of "dad" and grow from a daughter into a woman. If she is to be her own woman with her own life, she needs to get out of this no-win triangle. The same may be true for you.

If you're like Bonnie or Kendra, you probably describe yourself as independent, but you're really afraid of being dependent, of letting your neediness result in giving up too much of yourself. Ironically, dependency is a real danger for you in the Split Self Affair. Your life is on hold while you wait for your lover to leave his spouse. When he is stuck, you may even go so far as to call his wife, trying to persuade her to let him go. If your attempts to pry him loose from his wife fail, you may become discouraged enough to consider extricating yourself from the situation. To do so you will have to explore your issues around dependency and emotional vulnerability. These issues have to do with your conflicting desire to be taken care of and your fear of not being in control.

Taking Another Look at Your Life. It is hard to take responsibility for your own life after having so much given to you. You have to be pretty miserable to consider giving up the loving attention and the goodies—and your dreams. However, when you find yourself playing out the same patterns again and again, and you realize you're not getting on with your own life; it's time to reexamine what you really want, such as children or marriage. If being the third party is getting you down, take a new look at your situation to see if you are willing to make changes to get your life on a more satisfying course.

- What aspects of your relationship do you value?
- What are the hard parts for you?
- What's your timetable?
- What are your fears?
- What price would you say you have you paid so far?
- Has any of this shifted as you've encountered major changes in your life, such as the death of a parent?
- What is your gut feeling right now about where you are in your life? If you decide that you are comfortable enough, check yourself out again in six months.

Making Changes. If you are not comfortable, then it's time to get to work on yourself. It's not just your married partner who is split inside. You are similar in that you're a good girl on the surface, but a rebellious and somewhat defiant side of you is hidden—sometimes even from yourself. The work you need to do is much like the work that the other members of the triangle must do: face your reality, understand why you're settling for only a piece of the pie, resolve your issues around dependency and intimacy, develop new patterns of being honest and responsible for yourself, and learn to give yourself, including that rebellious self, a voice. These are the changes that will expand your life choices.

Some women choose—actively or by default—to stick it out for the rest of their lives as the Other Woman. Naomi almost did that. Divorced, Naomi got seriously involved with Jerry, a married man with three grown kids. They were intensely wrapped up in each other for almost four years until Jerry had a heart attack. Jerry's wife finally put her foot down and announced that she wasn't going to take care of him and he'd have to find another place to live unless he ended it with Naomi. The heart attack had scared Jerry so he readily agreed. However he didn't keep his word. He continued to call Naomi periodically, and occasionally they got together. Naomi hung on for another seven years, waiting for Jerry's calls and hanging on to the hope that he would leave his wife for her. Early in their affair Naomi had put her friends and activities on the back burner. By the time she got to therapy, she was pretty well isolated and increasingly depressed.

Naomi's therapist helped her pay attention to her pain and anger, feelings that she'd been suppressing all her life. The most difficult issue for Naomi was to risk exposing her vulnerable self, without freaking out. Gradually she found her own strengths and was ready to put Jerry aside. Three years later she married an available man and they've worked out a good relationship. She's no longer on a pedestal. She proclaims, "I don't need or want to be on anyone else's pedestal any more. Living on fantasies turned out to be a starvation diet. I know now how to take care of myself. My husband doesn't have to make me feel OK, and I know I won't put up with empty promises ever again. Of course, I love it when he does little things for me, and I like to do those things for him too, but we can both deal with reality, even when we don't agree. Sometimes I can't believe what I put up with. But that person is gone. No more 'little miss nurse.'"

When the Affair Continues Until Death. Some women choose to remain the Other Woman for as long as life allows. The shame and secrecy around affairs makes it hard for bereaved Other Women to find emotional support. Their loss is not seen as legitimate. They are outside, looking from a distance at the rituals designed to make saying good-bye easier for family and friends.

Fran is an exception. Fran continued her affair with Peter for eleven years. She spent a great deal of time with him during the week and on weekends (Peter's wife went along with his pattern of being gone a lot). Fran and Peter had a life together that included doing things with friends. As the Other Woman, Fran is somewhat unusual because she didn't sacrifice her friendships and activities nor did she hide her affair. Her pattern is reminiscent of the mistress system that is accepted still in many countries and operates here more covertly. She stayed in the affair despite Peter's inability to leave his wife, because she got the kind of attention and affection she craved, and she doubted whether at age thirty-nine she could find a man who would make her feel as lovable as Peter did. Neither had she sacrificed her support system.

Then Peter developed heart problems. She couldn't go to the hospital because his wife and his kids were there all the time. While he recuperated at home after open-heart surgery she had little contact with him. Mutual friends kept her posted on his condition, and he called her when he could. When Peter was able they resumed their old patterns. But then Peter was diagnosed with cancer and was told it was terminal. In his final days Fran wasn't able to be with him, and she didn't think it was fitting to attend his funeral. She handled her need for grieving and support by having her own memorial service for Peter, inviting all their mutual friends. Since she has maintained her friendships, Fran's job of rebuilding her life is not as difficult as for those Other Women whose only close relationship was with their affair partner.

When You Continue the Affair

Remember that his wife is not your problem. He is the one who is split inside and who is playing it out by attempting to choose between his wife and you. This problem is his, and you can't solve it for him. Keep these principles in mind:

- Keep your friendships. Don't let yourself get isolated.
- Recognize that you have issues to resolve and get to work on them.
- Keep your career going. Work usually provides opportunities for achievement and for social contacts, as well as for earning money and benefits.
- Consider whether you want a full-time committed relationship or whether you are comfortable enough being the third party.

The Exit Affair and You

Participation in an Exit Affair holds all the early exhilaration that is typical of serious affairs. The chemistry is intoxicating, the time together exciting, and the shared sense of purpose in helping your married partner through the separation process provides a bond. It's tempting for the third party to believe that this is the real thing, that you are the main course, especially when your affair partner does end the marriage. In a few cases this will be true, but in most of these affairs, you're the appetizer. The affair usually ends once the formerly married partner feels free enough to explore life as a single.

The affair is the justification for leaving the marriage, rather than the reason. It's about moving away from a negative, rather than toward a positive and lasting relationship. It's a serious relationship while it lasts, but since its purpose lies in ending the marriage, the affair seldom has the staying power to last more than six to eight months past the separation.

In Exit Affairs, single third parties are usually women. Single men seem less likely to choose an about-to-be-separated woman for an affair partner. Possibly this is because single men who want a relationship are more apt to pick a single woman, and those single men who are commitment phobic may prefer a married woman with family obligations rather than an about-to-be divorced woman who may soon make demands.

Gina, thirty-two years old and divorced ten years ago after a one-year marriage, was there for Nate starting six months before he left his wife. She listened to his reasons for wanting to leave and championed his decision; she let him know how attractive he was; and she supported him emotionally as he took the steps to end his marriage. She was surprised when five months after Nate left his wife, he wanted to go out with the guys. Within the next couple of months Nate was into the singles scene and broke off the relationship with Gina. She protested, "What am I? A nothing? Here I help him through the worst period of his life, and he can't wait to get out there and start partying—without me!"

If you're in Gina's position, expect this affair to end and plan accordingly. Keep your own life in good repair, with friends and work that you value. When the affair does end, let yourself go through a grieving process, rather than pretending it doesn't matter or trying to stuff your feelings away because they're so painful.

Even if this affair ends, you can use it to work on your issues. Consider whether the type of person you've chosen is part of a bigger pattern. Did prior partners disappoint or dump you in a similar way? If so, what is your old baggage that's getting in the way of choosing a different type of person, perhaps someone who takes better care of himself and who takes responsibility for his choices? What are your blind spots when you begin a relationship? For example, are you especially susceptible to someone who is charming, or are you hooked by challenges to prove you're OK? Do you find yourself doing all the work in each relationship you have? As you answer these questions, you can begin to work on the issues you have identified. See Chapter Six for guidance on identifying old baggage and developing the skills of intimacy.

Pregnancy: Upping the Ante

Affairs have been the source of conception for many children over the centuries. Some children are born to women married to someone other than the father; others are born to unmarried women. Many such pregnancies are aborted. With single third parties, pregnancy occurs most often in Split Self and Exit Affairs.

Julie, a single woman, observed, "I don't know how I could be so stupid." On deeper exploration she began to realize that her fantasies had been in charge. "Wouldn't it be nice. . . . Maybe we can have a family together. . . . What's to be, will be." She had abandoned responsibility for herself without quite admitting to herself that's what she was doing. Now that she is pregnant it looks very different. Sam is very supportive but he is in no position to marry her. He sort of likes the idea of fathering a baby, as long as his wife doesn't find out. But Julie is going to need child support if she has the baby, and that means Sam's wife would know, and probably so would everybody at work. Julie doesn't really want an abortion, but her job entails a great deal of travel and she can't care for a baby and keep her job. Yet she has to work to survive. Julie is in the classic double bind, with no *good* options.

Claire is a bit different. Over the three years she's been involved with Tom, he has promised Claire that he will move in with her and marry her as soon as he gets free of his wife. Claire is tired of waiting, and unsure about Tom's promises. She decided to speed things along, thinking "If I get pregnant, he'll have to leave." She's six months pregnant now and Tom still hasn't left. Tom's wife learned of Claire's pregnancy two months ago, but she's making no moves to kick Tom out. Claire is getting angry at Tom. Tom is feeling pushed from both sides, and being the Split Self he is, he still can't muster up the wherewithal to leave his wife. He's even beginning to have doubts about Claire as he sees how angry and demanding she is becoming. That's not the Claire he fell in love with. Often a pregnancy kills the affair as well as the marriage.

Serious Affairs: How Does It All Turn Out?

When you're involved in a serious affair you wonder: will it continue or will it end? Will it remain an affair or will you get married? What are the possibilities for your affair? It's possible that you might get married. Or you may decide to end the affair after using it to understand and address your unfinished business. Or your partner may do some work on himself and decide to end either the marriage or the affair, or both. Either of you may end the affair for other reasons, such as moving to another state. Or if it's a Split Self situation, your affair and your partner's marriage may continue along parallel paths until one or another of you dies.

You ask, "Can this affair ever work out?" In a small number of situations, the affair does become the marriage. To make it a successful marriage will take a tremendous amount of work, because you start with some strikes against you. You are forever linked by the affair, and that raises issues of trust between the two of you. Your relationship was built on your interlocking fantasies. Real life often turns out to be quite different, with its dailyness, its demands, and its disappointments. A critical area of work for you as a couple will be shifting from a relationship based almost exclusively on a positive emotional connection to one that also incorporates responsibility and honesty in facing conflicts, and requires that you each give yourself a voice about the tough stuff. Chapter Eight will guide you in completing the emotional work of ending the marriage. Chapter Six provides an outline of the work involved in building a healthy marriage.

Brief Affairs

Brief affairs range from those that appear safe when you are feeling vulnerable to low-demand affairs to sexual addiction. These brief affairs don't have the same mesmerizing power as a serious affair, but they do have the thrill of the conquest or the reassurance that someone finds you attractive, and some brief creature comforts. They also entail a high risk of catching a sexually transmitted disease. Loving or being loved usually isn't part of the picture.

Affairs for Safety's Sake

If you're just embarking on the social scene after leaving your spouse, you might deliberately choose someone who is married as insurance against remarrying before you're ready, or to protect against letting yourself fully care about someone. It's likely that you don't yet trust yourself to make good decisions, you're afraid of accommodating to a partner's wishes (you did so for years), or you picture yourself as becoming too dependent for your own good. Your married affair partner is unavailable a good part of the time and unable to make as many demands as a single might, thus freeing you from having to set boundaries you are not sure you can set.

Judy, recently separated from her intense and inflexible husband, got involved with Carl, married and in Judy's words, "a nice person." She said, "Carl's safe, and he can't make any demands on me. He's good to me—he's not intimidating like Walt." Judy had become strong enough to leave Walt, but she feared that she couldn't stand her ground with a single man who was free to make demands. Once Judy gets her feet on the ground as a single and learns to give herself a voice, she won't need or want to limit herself to married men.

Being the Third Party When You Want a Low-Demand Relationship

Many singles who grew up in dysfunctional families want attention and affection, but in their experience an ongoing relationship exacts too high a price, so they settle for brief interludes. In some cases, the single's primary relationship is with a career; casual relationships are relegated to leftover time and serious people-relationships are not part of the plan. Affairs are ideal, keeping you safe from pressures for commitment without having to be a total hermit, and leaving you with time for work. You may be satisfied with this for years, but when you begin to feel that something is missing, start looking at those aspects of intimacy that frighten you. You'll probably need professional help to learn how to let yourself get close.

Past traumas, such as childhood abuse, may also keep you wanting some built-in distance in a relationship. Here too, an affair seems to provide those safeguards: the married person isn't free to overwhelm you, and you have leverage against mistreatment: the secret of the affair.

Heavy career demands supersede committed relationships for some singles. You may find interludes are easier, requiring less time and energy during periods of extreme stress or the eighty-hour weeks required to climb the ladder in your company. Constant business travel also makes it difficult to pursue a serious relationship, and you may substitute brief affairs instead. Married people are attractive partners in these affairs because they tend to be "low maintenance."

Singles and Sexual Addiction

Sexual addiction, the compulsive use of sex to fill up inner emptiness, is another type of affair in which some singles participate. If you are having a series of brief affairs or one-night stands with married people (and probably with other singles as well), you probably don't know what a good relationship is or whether you want a continuing relationship. Inside, you feel empty much of the time. When you are pursuing a sexual conquest, however, you don't feel so empty. If you're a man, you may cover up by bragging to your friends about your conquests. If you're a woman you're more likely to be conscious of shame about your behavior so you don't say much to your friends.

Profiles of Singles with Compulsive Sexual Patterns

- It matters little who your affair partner is.
- You use sex to fill your emptiness or numb your pain.
- You've lost track of the number of sexual partners you've had.
- You are preoccupied with the pursuit of sex.
- You are likely to have a second addiction.
- Your original family was abusive and confused about sexual boundaries.

How Compulsive Sexual Patterns Develop in Singles

Kyle's way of coping with the pain of childhood abuse was to medicate himself with sex. He was the kid who was always being ignored or being hit. He tried to stay out of the way of his father's heavy hand, and sought attention elsewhere. His mother didn't protect him—she was scared of his father too. From an early age, he masturbated for consolation. As he matured physically, he discovered the excitement of the sexual conquest. The conquest was as important as the sex in filling his emptiness and numbing his pain—at least for the moment. He's had well over a hundred brief affairs and one-night stands but his inner emptiness continues to gnaw. To give up his pattern of sexual seduction, Kyle will need to reclaim his right to his own feelings, so that he no longer feels empty inside. That means he will have to deal with all the suppressed pain of his childhood—no fun, but healing. Recovering from Sexual Addiction is discussed in Chapter Seven.

Singles who are sexual addicts are less anchored in the world than are married sexual addicts. The married addict has a spouse and maybe kids at home. Family members may be ashamed of the addict and have mixed feelings about him, but they're there. Single sexual addicts seldom have much of a support system—maybe some other addicts to join with, or acquaintances who don't really know the person inside the addict. It's lonely being a sexual addict.

Singles who engage in compulsive sex are less likely to seek help than those in other types of affairs, but when they do, it is because they don't like their lives or themselves and want to make changes. Just as with alcohol addiction, change is possible.

Summary

Single women and men become involved as the third party in affairs, serious or brief, for a variety of reasons having to do with unfinished business from the past. The duration of these affairs ranges from a single chance encounter to a decades-long relationship. Many singles continue to choose a partner who is married. For others, participation in an affair with a married partner is a way station. Consider this chapter the beginning of a search for finding your own story—and for deciding whether to change how your own next chapters are written.

Chapter Twelve

Making Peace, Moving On

Out of the pain and upheaval comes the
opportunity to forgive and to live.

An affair is a critical point in your life journey, whether you are
the betrayed or betraying spouse. The aftermath takes time to sort
through and resolve. From the moment the affair is initiated you
both embark on a process that has several phases. First comes the
siren song of the affair, complete with fantasy, romance, and a
nagging discomfort or outright guilt for the betraying partner.
With the discovery of the affair, the betrayed spouse experiences
shock and moves quickly to obsession. Then you both begin to
understand the meaning of the affair in the larger context of your
personal history and the history of your marriage. Next is the
rebuilding process, which includes developing the skills of
intimacy and healing old wounds. In essence, you are learning
how to be alive and adult in your emotional life. Finally
there comes a point when you're ready to forgive and move
beyond the affair.

Forgiveness is the last step in making peace after an affair. It is
the symbolic marker that moves the affair from your present to your
past. The paths to forgiveness are varied. You may reach this point
together or apart, alone or as part of a new couple, in a year or after
many years. Your journey will encompass pain and anger, joy and
excitement, change and loss. If you are growing, you will struggle
with yourself more than with your spouse. In the course of your
struggle you will move toward being a real adult. No quick and easy

route exists. The important thing is to continue using your new skills. Life is too messy if you don't.

A Perspective on Forgiving

Let's look at what forgiving is about. Back when the affair had just surfaced, both of you were busy trying to make sense of your situation. You were trying to come up with a story that connected your old life to the reality of the affair. Now you're on the other end of this process, trying to put some of the last pieces in place so that you can move on. In each stage of the process you rework your story about where you've been and how you understand where you are now. Forgiveness is a capstone to the story of the affair. It validates your experience of the affair and puts it in a larger perspective. The affair becomes one of the stories that make up your marriage and your life; it's no longer *the* story.

Acknowledgment is always a major aspect of forgiving. Forgiving means acknowledging losses and mistakes, pain and sadness, regrets and joys. The pain that stemmed from the problems between you was so intense because the two of you had so many important ties that were disrupted. Those ties have value of their own and need to be acknowledged. This means talking about the importance of your marriage, the experiences that were good between the two of you, and the experiences that were difficult. Hearing each other's pain is in itself a major act of forgiveness.

For Couples Who Stay Together: Are You Ready to Forgive?

Forgiveness is easiest when you've worked on your issues and you've chosen to stay together. You've gone through a process of getting to know yourselves and each other in new ways. You've lost your idealism and naïveté about marriage, and replaced it with a healthy reality that keeps you grounded in the present.

Early on you were impatient to get to the point of forgiving. By the time you're ready to forgive, you've done so much work that your impatience is long since gone. In its place is the knowledge that each of you has taken a long and difficult journey and there's no need to rush. You can forgive and be forgiven when you're ready, rather than seeking a quick fix for your desperation.

Some couples are afraid that once they forgive, they can't ever talk about the affair again; in other words, if they forgive, they have to forget. But you're never going to forget—and it's better if you don't. The memory of the affair serves as a reminder of what can go wrong when you don't take care of things. Forgiving frees you up to talk more easily, without wondering if the affair will be held over your head once again. You might even voluntarily refer to the affair, or use it as personal shorthand, as in "before the affair—" meaning "back when we were sweeping everything under the rug and not dealing with each other." Carla and Ben, who in Chapter Five were struggling with her obsession, found later on that they could enjoy some rueful humor about his affair.

When is it time to forgive and be forgiven? How do you know you're ready? You know you're ready to forgive each other when:

- There are no longer any angels or devils.
- You let go of obsessing awhile back.
- You have heard and acknowledged each other's pain about the affair.
- You understand why the affair happened and what it meant in your marriage.
- You trust yourself and each other again—or for the first time.
- You have learned and are using the skills of intimacy: paying attention to your feelings, giving yourself a voice, being honest, owning responsibility for yourself, and trusting yourself enough to risk being emotionally vulnerable with your partner.

- You have learned how to achieve the positive things you want, such as feeling alive, without betraying your spouse.
- You can talk about the affair without feeling overwhelmed or reacting strongly. The affair is not controlling the present, it's part of your history.
- The stuff under the rug has been examined in the light of day, and dealt with.
- You each feel secure in your own right.
- A spirit of equity and reciprocity is present.

Forgiving is itself a process, not just an event. It incorporates understanding why the affair occurred, acknowledging the pain it caused, asking to be forgiven, and renegotiating the relationship. As you move toward forgiving and being forgiven, you will engage in heartfelt conversations with each other about where you've been, where you are now, and where you are going. You'll share your feelings and your thoughts as you acknowledge the good, the bad, and the important.

Are there loose ends about the affair that need to be discussed and put to rest? If so, this is the time. Don't bury them in an attempt to "make nice." Does other unfinished business between you need closure now? Keep in mind that it's not a matter of finishing everything off for all time. If you and your marriage are growing, you will always have some new challenge in your relationship to address. Right now, however, your task is to make peace with the affair and the factors that led to it, and to move toward the future with different patterns and expectations.

Reexamining your expectations for your marriage, and talking about what you can and cannot commit to is a major piece of preparing for forgiveness. Ben, for example, committed to telling Carla whenever he was bothered by something between them, rather than acting it out. Carla committed to voicing whatever was bothering her, rather than stuffing it out of sight. Both agreed to consult with each other before making individual plans with friends, but neither believed it was appropriate to ask permission to see friends. Take sufficient time so that your discussions can be rich and detailed. In so doing you will become closer emotionally.

When you both feel that the affair is truly over and your marriage is on track, each of you can ask the other to forgive you. Asking is important; it is an aspect of taking responsibility for yourself and your part in the marital difficulties. You might ask very simply, "Will you forgive me for the pain I have caused you? Or you might ask, "Will you forgive me for keeping myself a secret for so long?" You can choose words that have meaning to you and to your spouse.

You might want to acknowledge the importance of the affair in changing the course of your relationship. You could even begin to think of the affair as a gift—a gift that turned your marriage around. This was true for Rob and Diane. Before her affair, Rob's usual response to Diane was "Yes dear, whatever you want." When the affair surfaced, Diane told Rob she didn't think she wanted to stay married to him, but she agreed to work on the marriage when he pleaded for another chance. As they happily reviewed all the changes they had made in the past year, Rob said of the affair, "You really got something started!"

For many of those who are religious, a full sense of forgiveness also requires some meaningful contact with their religious organization. For Catholics, this would include the Sacrament of Reconciliation. For those of different faiths, resolving the affair at a spiritual level might mean meeting with a minister, rabbi, or other spiritual leader or participating in a significant religious ritual.

Forgiving Each Other When Your Marriage Has Ended

Forgiving each other is just as important for couples whose marriage has ended as for those who are still together after an affair. Forgiving frees you to move ahead without lingering resentment or grievances about the past. Issues that need resolution, such as a traumatic event that never got talked about, can be finished off as well.

You won't be ready to think about forgiving for several years after you separate. Instead, your energy will be devoted to grieving over the end of your marriage, to coping with the disruption of divorce, and eventually to building your life on firmer ground. Along the way you will get a clearer understanding of how you contributed to the marital problems, including making enough space for the affair. You'll probably need a minimum of two years after separating before you're ready. Most couples whose marriage ends with an affair need four to five years or longer to be ready.

Most of the criteria for readiness listed earlier for couples who stay together are good ones for you to apply as well. The criteria for trust are a little different. Since you have not been up close and personal with each other for awhile, you may not be clear about your ex's level of trustworthiness. You will know however, whether he or she has been a loving parent to your children, whether the terms of your divorce have been honored, and whether your ex talks to you with respect.

Your willingness to risk talking at a deep level with your ex depends on your readiness to forgive. When you are ready, you will need to trust that you can handle whatever comes your way; especially emotions that are aroused in you. That means if your ex should revert to old and unpleasant behavior, you can stay out of the old patterns. It also means that if you're disappointed after your discussion with your ex you'll be disappointed but not crushed. If both of you have done your work, your trust level will probably be much greater than it was prior to the affair, even if you are divorced.

When you feel ready for closure with your ex, ask yourself what is unfinished between the two of you. For example, Mary had wondered recently why she and her ex had never talked about the death of their infant son, who was born six weeks prematurely. She invited her ex to join her in talking to a therapist about this painful but buried aspect of their life together. The therapist helped them share their pain at losing their son, and explore the reasons they hadn't felt able to talk about it earlier. It became apparent that the inability to share their grief was the turning point that culminated in divorce. By talking this through, they were able to get a clearer perspective on their life together, including the Exit Affair that had been used to end the marriage.

You don't always need a therapist's help. When you're ready to forgive and be forgiven, you can arrange to get together with your former mate to gain closure, or you can take advantage of an unforeseen opportunity that presents itself. Lydia arranged an opportunity seven years after she and her former husband Bill parted. She invited Bill over for brunch when he was in town to see the children. Their divorce had been a hostile one, with lots of lit-igation, but things had been quiet for a couple of years now. Lydia followed her gut sense that she was ready to make peace with Bill. She had less in common with Bill than ever, but the growing up she had done made her ready to treat Bill as well as she treated other acquaintances. After talking about their children and catch-ing each other up on friends and family, Lydia said quietly, "There's been a lot of water under the bridge. I'm sorry it turned out this way." Bill replied, "I know. I'm sorry too." Lydia had tears in her eyes as Bill responded. Although the words were simple, they were emotionally momentous for Lydia and Bill and gave each of them a sense of closure on their marriage.

For most couples who divorce after an affair, forgiveness comes sooner than for Lydia and Bill. It happened spontaneously for Melva, whose Exit Affair two years ago marked the end of her mar-riage to Jim. Melva called Jim and asked to come over to talk about changes in the health insurance for their children. She shifted almost immediately into talking nostalgically about their marriage, and her sadness at what had been lost. She noted that she hadn't changed her mind about ending the marriage, but went on to talk about the good times they had shared with friends and family, the joy they got from their children, and other fond memories of their life together. Jim joined her in remembering and they ended up talking for over two hours about their good times and about the difficulties that they hadn't known how to address. Before they finished, Melva speculated whether they would still be married if they had known earlier what they knew now. They were back to being real people in each other's eyes; no longer the betraying spouse or the insensitive and controlling partner. In effect, Melva and Jim were mutually validating their life together—and in so doing, forgiving each other and bringing closure to the story of their marriage.

You may wonder if it's possible to be friends with your former spouse. Yes, if you were friends before, it's possible that you could become friends again—after you forgive and reach closure with each other. It's easier if the affair partner is no longer in the picture.

Forgiving When You Alone Are Ready to Forgive

Sometimes forgiveness is not mutual. Your former partner may be unable or unwilling to forgive. You however, are ready to shed the burden of anger and resentment, and want to put the past in the past.

You can do so. Start by acknowledging your dreams, studying your mistakes, and grieving over your losses. Then feel your way in identifying what you want to say to your former spouse—not necessarily what you would say, but what you want to say right now. As you become clear, write it down in the form of a letter to your former mate. Don't worry about form or grammar right now—this edition is for your eyes only. You can be as hurt or as angry as you want. Grab your feelings and get them on paper. If you have a lot to say about the affair, you're not yet ready for closure. Nonetheless, keep writing. It gives you a safe place to dump your emotional overload. Stash what you've written where no one will find it. Continue to write as the spirit moves you.

When you feel ready, read through what you have written to get a clearer sense of the emotional journey you have been on. Begin to focus on what you actually need to say to your ex in order to achieve closure for yourself. It needs to be short, to the point, and come from your emotional self. Madeline, whose husband, Jack, had an Exit Affair, has moved on to the point that she is indignant rather than angry about how she was treated. She decided to send the following letter to Jack. It is a statement of empowerment for herself as well as closure with Jack.

> Dear Jack,
>
> As you know, I have been very hurt and angry at your betrayal and abandonment of me. I deserved better from you. We started out with such high hopes. I'm sorry it has come to this. I wish you well.
>
> Madeline

What do you do if you're not a writer, or if sending such a letter might stir up trouble? One man described visualizing his wife, then making her die in his mind, grieving for her, and then burying her. This was an internal process for him at first. When he was ready to bury her, he decided to actually bury the picture he had kept of her. He felt sad, but freed, much as if she had died after a long illness.

Many other ways of reaching closure exist. You can use your creative self to decide how to symbolically address the betrayal you experienced, reclaim your sense of empowerment, and attain closure for yourself.

Will You Have Another Affair?

If you've moved through all the phases of resolving an affair, and learned the skills of intimacy, you're unlikely to have another affair. Being honest and taking responsibility for yourself doesn't permit having an affair.

Could you slip? Well, it's possible that you could go back to your old patterns. That would be hard, though, because you know so much more about yourself. You probably can't kid yourself the way you could in the past. It's useful to talk with your partner about how you might sabotage yourself by withholding your emotions or engaging in boundary drift. You can't rationalize nearly as well when you've already put your finger on patterns that would indicate that you're getting away from being your responsible self.

A good marriage takes hard work. Sometimes the temptation arises to just take it easy. It's OK to take it easy for an evening, but even then you need to be conscious and take responsibility for the choices you are making.

Successful Affairs

Among those whose lives are touched by an affair, there are marriages that succeed, individuals who succeed, and affairs that succeed. Successful individuals and successful marriages are those that are vital, dwelling in the present, thriving on the joys and the challenges, and addressing the losses and mistakes that occur. These partners have developed an approach to life that enables them to delight in intimacy, to keep problems in perspective, to resolve differences, and to invest in themselves and in others. This kind of success is possible whether or not the original marriage survived.

It may seem curious to think about a successful affair. Yet some affairs are extremely successful. What makes an affair successful? A successful affair:

- Brings you to consciousness.
- Sets off a positive chain reaction.
- Is the catalyst for getting to work on yourself and your marriage.
- Rules out the need to escape because you are facing your issues instead.
- Teaches you that you can feel alive *and* act responsibly.
- Results in earning respect—from yourself as well as your spouse (or ex-spouse).
- Is part of your history, but is not controlling the present.

- Makes you rethink your steps along the way so that you are more aware of the choices you're making now.
- Has taught you to be honest, responsible, vocal, and vulnerable with your partner about your feelings and your thoughts.

Healing from an affair gives you a different perspective on affairs as well as on yourself and your marriage. Here are some of my favorite comments by those who survived and thrived after an affair:

"I can look back and see how we were making the bed for this affair."

"In the affair I was learning about another part of myself— that's what I fell in love with. And now I can share that part of myself with you."

"Our marriage was one hell of a shell. I thank God for the affair, or we'd still be in that shell."

"Joan did us a favor. She woke us up to the fact that *we* were crumbling. Now we've got *we* back, better than before."

This chapter closes with the following poem, written by a man who had an affair. He writes as if his wife is speaking to him.

Love Me Honest Sir[1]

*Build me a house with windows and skylights so I can always
      see inside.*
Privacy in the bathrooms is OK as long as I can see the light.
Make the foundation deep and out of rock.
High ceilings, no small rooms or halls for hiding clutter.
Make it so all the windows open for lots of light and air.
But only one door with a key.
So even if always open I will know who or what goes in there.
Then move your heart in,
And love me like that.

Notes

Preface

1. Hite, Shere, *The Hite Report on Male Sexuality*. New York: Knopf, 1978, p. 142.

   Creaturo, Barbara, "An Intimate Look at Adultery," *Cosmopolitan*, Nov. 1982, pp. 233–235, 286–288.

   Scarf, Maggie, *Intimate Partners*. New York: Random House, 1987.

   Lawson, Annette, *Adultery: An Analysis of Love and Betrayal*. New York: Basic Books, 1988, pp. 74–75.

Chapter 1

1. Kasl, Charlotte Davis, *Women, Sex, and Addiction*. New York: Ticknor & Fields, 1989, p. 113.

Chapter 2

1. Boodman, Sandra G., "Study Finds That Bad News Is Better Than Uncertainty." *Washington Post*, November 17, 1992, Health Section, p. 5.

2. Charny, Israel, and Sivan Parnass, "The Impact of Extramarital Relationships on the Continuation of Marriages." *Journal of Sex & Marital Therapy*, 1995, *21*(2), 100–115.

Chapter 3

1. Pope, Alexander, "Essay on Criticism."

Chapter 4

1. Bachman, Ronet, *Violence Against Women: A National Crime Victimization Survey Report*. Washington, D.C.: Bureau of Justice Statistics, U.S. Department of Justice, January 1994.

   Dawson, John M., and Patrick A. Langan, *Murder in Families*. Bureau of Justice Statistics Special Report, Washington, D.C.: U.S. Department of Justice, July 1994.

2. Eckhardt, Christopher I., and Jerry L. Deffenbacher, "Diagnosis of Anger Disorders," in *Anger Disorders: Definition, Diagnosis, and Treatment*, Howard Kassinove, Editor. Washington, D.C.: Taylor & Francis, 1995, p. 30.

   Tsytsarev, Sergei V., and Gustavo R. Grodnitzky, "Anger and Criminality," in *Anger Disorders*, p. 104.

   Meloy, J. Reid, *Violent Attachments*. Northvale, N.J.: Aronson, 1992, pp. 193–210.

3. Dawson, John M., and Patrick A. Langan, *Murder in Families*. Bureau of Justice Statistics Special Report, Washington, D.C.: U.S. Department of Justice, July 1994.

4. Valentine, Paul, "Staff Sergeant Discharged in Sex Scandal." *Washington Post*, October 29, 1997, p. A18.

   "Female B-52 Pilot Charged with Adultery, Other Offenses." *Washington Post*, February 22, 1997, p. A6.

   "Pentagon Probes Guard General's Relationship to a Subordinate." *Washington Post*, November 8, 1998, p. A18.

5. Johnston, Janet, and Linda E. G. Campbell, "Parent-Child Relationships in Domestic Violence Families Disputing Custody." *Family and Conciliation Courts Review*, 1993, *31*(3), 282–298.

6. Johnston and Campbell, "Parent-Child Relationships."

Chapter 5

No notes.

Chapter 6

1. Lerner, Harriet Goldhor, *The Dance of Anger.* New York: HarperCollins, 1985.

Chapter 7

1. Carnes, Patrick, *Don't Call It Love: Recovery from Sexual Addiction.* New York: Bantam, 1991, p. 35.

2. Milkman, Harvey B., and Stanley Sunderwirth, *Craving for Ecstasy: The Consciousness and Chemistry of Escape.* San Francisco: New Lexington Press, 1986.

3. Carnes, Patrick, *A Gentle Path Through the Twelve Steps: For All People in the Process of Recovery.* Minneapolis, Minn.: CompCare, 1989.

4. Beattie, Melody, *Co-Dependent No More.* Center City, Minn.: Hazelden, 1987.

Chapter 8

No notes.

Chapter 9

No notes.

Chapter 10

1. Depner, Charlene E., E. Victor Leino, and Amy Chun, "Interparental Conflict and Child Adjustment: A Decade Review and Meta-Analysis." *Family and Conciliation Courts Review,* 1992, 3, 323–341.

Grych, John, and Frank Fincham, "Marital Conflict and Children's Adjustment: A Cognitive-Contextual Framework." *Psychological Bulletin*, 1990, *108*, 267–290.

Johnston, Janet R., "High Conflict Divorce." *Future of Children: Children and Divorce*, 1994, *4*(1), 165–182.

Emery, Robert E., "Interparental Conflict and the Children of Discord and Divorce." *Psychological Bulletin*, 1982, *92*, 310–330.

2. Ricci, Isolina, *Mom's House, Dad's House* (2nd edition). New York: Simon & Schuster, 1997.

Chapter 11

1. Viorst, Judith, *Necessary Losses*. New York: Simon & Schuster, 1986, p. 103.

Chapter 12

1. Price, Dennis, "Love Me Honest Sir." Unpublished manuscript, February 25, 1997.

Recommended Reading

The following books are ones that have been especially useful for many of my clients. Some were originally recommended by my clients, others I have discovered and recommended. In reading, remember that you don't have to read the entire book, and you don't have to read the chapters in order. Read the first chapter, and then, if you wish, go directly to the chapter that relates to where you are now, before reading the other chapters that have meaning for you.

Affairs

Brown, Emily M. *Patterns of Infidelity and Their Treatment*. New York: Brunner/Mazel, 1991.

Fisher, Helen. *Anatomy of Love: The Natural History of Monogamy, Adultery and Divorce*. New York: Norton, 1992.

Lawson, Annette. *Adultery: An Analysis of Love and Betrayal*. New York: Basic Books, 1988.

Lusterman, Don-David. *Infidelity: A Survival Guide*. Oakland, Calif.: New Harbinger, 1998.

Reibstein, Janet, and Martin Richards. *Sexual Arrangements: Marriage and the Temptation of Infidelity*. New York: Scribner, 1993.

Spring, Janis Abrahms. *After the Affair*. New York: HarperCollins, 1996.

Vaughan, Peggy. *The Monogamy Myth: A Personal Handbook for Recovering from Affairs* (revised edition). New York: Newmarket Press, 1998.

Old Baggage

Bepko, Claudia. *Too Good for Her Own Good: Searching for Self and Intimacy in Important Relationships*. New York: HarperCollins, 1991.

Bradshaw, John. *Homecoming: Reclaiming and Championing Your Inner Child*. New York: Bantam Books, 1992.

Chernin, Kim. *The Woman Who Gave Birth to Her Mother*. New York: Viking, 1998.

Forward, Susan. *Toxic Parents*. New York: Bantam Books, 1990.

Goleman, Daniel. *Emotional Intelligence: Why It Can Matter More Than IQ*. New York: Bantam Books, 1995.

Harris, Maxine. *The Loss That Is Forever: The Lifelong Impact of the Early Death of a Mother or Father*. New York: Plume, 1995.

Miller, Alice. *The Drama of the Gifted Child*. New York: Basic Books, 1981.

Zoldbrod, Aline P. *Sex Smart*. Oakland, Calif.: New Harbinger, 1998.

Couple Relationships

DeAngelis, Barbara. *Are You the One for Me?* New York: Dell, 1992.

Gottman, John. *Why Marriages Succeed or Fail*. New York: Simon & Schuster, 1994.

Hendrix, Harville. *Getting the Love You Want: A Guide for Couples*. New York: HarperCollins, 1988.

Lerner, Harriet Goldhor. *The Dance of Anger*. New York: HarperCollins, 1985.

Lerner, Harriet Goldhor. *The Dance of Deception: Pretending and Truth-Telling in Women's Lives*. New York: HarperCollins, 1993.

Lerner, Harriet Goldhor. *The Dance of Intimacy*. New York: HarperCollins, 1989.

Markman, Howard, Scott Stanley, and Susan L. Blumberg. *Fighting for Your Marriage*. San Francisco: Jossey-Bass, 1994.

Pennebaker, James W. *Opening Up*. New York: Morrow, 1990.

Scarf, Maggie. *Intimate Partners: Patterns in Love and Marriage*. New York: Random House, 1987.

Divorce

Ahrons, Constance R. *The Good Divorce: Keeping Your Family Together When Your Marriage Comes Apart*. New York: HarperCollins, 1994.

Garrity, Carla B., and Mitchell A. Baris. *Caught in the Middle: Protecting the Children of High-Conflict Divorce*. San Francisco: New Lexington Press, 1994.

Gold, Lois. *Between Love and Hate: A Guide to Civilized Divorce*. New York: Plenum, 1992.

Kramer, Peter D. *Should You Leave?* New York: Scribner, 1997.

Lyster, Mimi E. *Child Custody: Building Agreements That Work*. Berkeley, Calif.: Nolo Press, 1995.

Ricci, Isolina. *Mom's House, Dad's House* (2nd edition). New York: Simon & Schuster, 1997.

Anger and Violence

Cullen, Murray, and Robert E. Freeman-Longo. *Men and Anger*. Brandon, Vt.: Safer Society Press, 1996.

Jones, Ann, and Susan Schechter. *When Love Goes Wrong*. New York: Harper-Collins, 1993.

McKay, Matthew, Peter D. Rogers, and Judith McKay. *When Anger Hurts*. Oakland, Calif.: New Harbinger, 1989.

Potter-Efron, Ron, and Pat Potter-Efron. *Letting Go of Anger*. Oakland, Calif.: New Harbinger, 1995.

Sexual Addiction

Anonymous. *Hope and Recovery: A Twelve Step Guide for Healing from Compulsive Sexual Behavior*. Minneapolis, Minn.: CompCare, 1987.

Carnes, Patrick. *Don't Call It Love*. New York: Bantam Books, 1991.

Carnes, Patrick. *A Gentle Path Through the Twelve Steps: For All People in the Process of Recovery*. Minneapolis, Minn.: CompCare, 1989.

Kasl, Charlotte Davis. *Women, Sex, and Addiction*. New York: Ticknor & Fields, 1989.

Forgiving

Casarjian, Robin. *Forgiveness: A Bold Choice for a Peaceful Heart*. New York: Bantam Books, 1992.

Smedes, Lewis B. *The Art of Forgiving*. New York: Ballantine, 1996.

Resources

This compilation of resources is designed to help you find professionals and organizations that can provide you with services, and to locate additional information that may help you as you work toward resolving your situation.

Finding Help on the Web

As you know, the Web is filled with treasure and trash. These are some of the treasures for people working toward resolution of an affair. Most of these sites have links to other sites that you will also want to explore. In addition, you can search the Web using keywords such as "extramarital affairs" or "infidelity."

www.affairs-help.com

www.itstessie.com (Religious)

www.vaughan-vaughan.com

www.pages.prodigy.com/divorceplus/div00.htm

Finding a Therapist

The following national organizations will provide you with a referral or will give you the phone number of the state organization that makes referrals.

American Association of Marriage and Family Therapists, (202) 452-0109

National Federation of Societies for Clinical Social Work, (703) 522-3866 or (800) 270-9739

National Association of Social Workers, (202) 408-8600

American Psychological Association, (202) 336-5500

American Association of Pastoral Counselors, (703) 385-6967

American Counseling Association, (703) 823-9800 or (800) 347-6647

Finding a Mediator

Academy of Family Mediators, (617) 674-2663; Web site: www.igc.org/afm

Local courts that handle custody disputes may offer mediation services.

Finding Help with Sexual Addiction

Sex Addicts Anonymous, (713) 869-4902

Sex and Love Addicts Anonymous, (617) 332-1845

Sexaholics Anonymous, (615) 331-6230; e-mail: saico@sa.org

S-Anon International Family Groups, (615) 833-3152; e-mail: sanon@sanon.org

Other Organizations

Your local hotlines. Call your local Mental Health Association, Community Mental Health Center, or Family Service Agency for the hotline number in your community.

Community Mental Health Centers. These organizations are publicly funded and usually offer emergency services, often on a twenty-four-hour basis.

About the Author

Emily M. Brown, LCSW, MSW, is founder and director of the Key Bridge Therapy & Mediation Center in Arlington, Virginia. As a clinical social worker, marriage and family therapist, and family mediator, she works with couples, individuals, and families regarding the underlying issues in marriage, divorce, and betrayal. She leads retreats for those who have experienced an affair and is increasingly called upon by corporations to consult about the issue of affairs in the workplace. She also trains mental health professionals throughout North America and in Europe to use the strategies she has developed for working successfully with the issues surrounding affairs.

Her book *Patterns of Infidelity and Their Treatment* is used as a guide by many therapists. She has also written numerous articles for therapists and for the general public on affairs and other aspects of marriage and divorce. She is frequently quoted in publications such as the *Readers' Digest*, the *Washington Post*, *USA Today*, *Ladies' Home Journal*, *Glamour*, *Cosmopolitan*, and *New Woman*. She has been featured on *Oprah*, *Donahue*, the *Today Show*, CNBC's *Real Personal*, the *Shirley Show* (in Canada), National Public Television, NPR's *Talk of the Nation*, and numerous other radio and television programs.

She encourages those who are struggling with an affair to face their chaotic feelings so that the affair, rather than being a tragedy, becomes a catalyst for positive change.

About the Affairs-Help Web Site

Readers are invited to visit my Web site, www.affairs-help.com, for information about affairs, workshops, and research, and to share their experiences on the bulletin boards. I would welcome any comments, reactions, and suggestions that readers care to offer about this book or about the Web site. You can reach me by following the links at www.affairs-help.com or sending e-mail to key-bridge-center@erols.com

Index